WHAT THE MEDIA WON'T TELL YOU ABOUT THE WAR IN SYRIA

ESSAYS

WASEEM KANJO

"Today I want to tell you three stories from my life. [...] The first story is about connecting the dots. [...] Of course it was impossible to connect the dots looking forward [...] but it was very, very clear looking backwards ten years later. Again, you can't connect the dots looking forward you can only connect them looking backwards so you have to trust that the dots will somehow connect in your future. [...] For the past 33 years I've looked in the mirror every morning and asked myself if today were the last day of my life what I want to do what I am about to do today and whenever the answer has been. [...] Remembering that I'll be dead soon is the most important tool I've ever encountered to help me make the big choices in life because almost everything all external expectations all pride all fear of embarrassment. [...] Remembering that you are going to die is the best way I know to avoid the trap of thinking you have something to lose. Don't be trapped by Dogma which is living with the results of other people's thinking. Don't let the noise of others opinions drown out your own."

Steve Jobs

Contents

FROM THE AUTHOR

What happened in Syria can easily be replicated in any other part of this world. The war became a product which is being reproduced and replicated. It is urgent that humanity understands what has really happened. It is also must understand how it happened and why so that we can stop this from consuming from our planet. It is like the flames of a dragon burning up one nation after another.

Reflecting on the essays in this book, the reader may begin to understand not only what has happened in Syria, but also what is currently happening in Yemen, Libya and soon in many other parts of this world.

Most of what follows comes from my personal experiences, stemming from the 30 years I lived in Syria before the war, and the two years after it started, in addition to my researches and what I have witnessed in Turkey and Europe.

After moving to Europe, I had a growing feeling that we were not being told everything about the war and that the media is selective about some of the information it allows us to hear. This was the reason I decided to write about it and to share my views and thoughts with you. It is principally what I saw and how that relates to what you think you already know.

Preface

More and more, the media covers every single event in this universe. There are barely any things that happen or even have yet to happen which our time's media doesn't cover. Most of what you read or watch in the media is true and almost 100% accurate. But HOW you're told the stories, and WHEN, there lies the manipulation!

When the word "war" is used, some glorious scenes might come to mind. Wars could be those historical battles, where strong young men meet to demonstrate their youth and strength, and where the leaders strive to show their intelligence. We all go to cinemas to watch films about such wars. We tell children stories about them. Thus, I find "war" far too romantic when I try to describe what happens in Syria. In this tragedy, no skills were demonstrated but turning hospitals, children, and civilians into piles of limbs and blood. The leaders of the fighter parties have barely met and hardly lost at all. They came back home at the end of the war, all safe, all winners, with enlarged pockets and full bank accounts, while millions of civilians were displaced. Unlimited stories of torture, unlimited limbs were cut, unlimited eyes were gouged out and heads were cut off. The war was not designed to fight for something. No land, raw material or strategic position was gained. It was not for fighting or winning. It was designed just to create the most tragic story in human history.

It is not only the number of victims that made this tragedy one of the ugliest wars in history[1]. What defines the Syrian war is that it happened at a time when the world was supposed to be "mature," with apparent sophisticated international law systems implemented by nations and organizations who assumed that such a war was no longer possible on this planet. The massacres in Rwanda or Kosovo happened before – while humanity was taking a "nap". Times had changed and the international community "came of age" and its ethics became clear enough to make such cases exist only in history books. At least, that is what the Syrians thought (or were led to believe).

The millions of demonstrators who headed out to the streets had enough reason to act against such corrupt and murderous regimes. However, they had enough reason before that as well and refrained from such steps for decades. They were not ignorant of their regime's ethics (or lack thereof) and its unlimited brutality. Actually, they have been aware of this regime and its allies' amoral standards since 1982, or even earlier. Neither were they so stupid that they miscalculated their arsenal versus their country's[2].

---

[1] Actually, many more terrible wars in history have killed even more victims, destroyed more property and lives, and lasted longer than the Syrian war.

[2] Before 2011, a hunting gun is the most lethal weapon a Syrian individual could own against a regime that was prepared to face Israel, backed unlimitedly by Russia, Iran, and many other

They took these steps relying mainly on the supposed "maturity" of the world's nations and organizations, including many outsider events which were completely out of the Syrians' influence3. However, and this is very important, this reliance didn't come spontaneously, rather it was carefully planned, and this point is critical to understanding exactly what happened. Declarations and promises by presidents like Obama, Erdogan, and European leadersi were systematic and clear. They were accompanied by serious work on the ground. Tracking these declarations across the years of crises leaves no doubt that they were not accidental, mistaken, or innocent4.

---

countries and semi-countries (like Hezbollah and plenty of radical sectarian and mercenary militias).

[3] Events like huge waves of incoming weapons and foreigners, besides financial and media factors, which I will describe thoroughly throughout the pages of this book.
See Reuters' Article on 22.11.2011 "Turkish PM calls on Syria's Assad to quit. While Turkey is opposed to outside intervention, it has met with Syrian opposition groups and allows them to meet in Turkish cities. It has also given refuge to Syrian army defectors but denies it is supporting an armed resistance. Turkish newspapers quoted officials at the weekend saying Turkey could set up a no-fly or buffer zone in Syrian territory to protect people from Assad's security forces, in order to head off a potential mass exodus of refugees from Syria.
Turkish Prime Minister Tayyip Erdogan called on Tuesday for Syria's president to step down and likened Damascus's crackdown on protesters to the tactics of Nazi Germany."
https://www.reuters.com/article/us-turkey-syria/turkish-pm-calls-on-syrias-assad-to-quit-idUSTRE7AL0WJ20111122
[4] Jeffrey Sachs, director of the Earth Institute at Columbia University: "This is a US mistake that started seven years ago. And I remember the day when President Obama said: "Assad

Was it then a "conspiracy" against the Syrian regime? Here is the mysterious part of the story: the regime of Assad was a part of this "conspiracy" not a bystander or a contradicting force. All of his acts and reactions supported the mission of this conspiracy and aided it. The media coverage explained the unjustified violence by Assad's regime as a sort of fascism, sadism or political stupidity. As you read further you will understand why this explanation is not sufficient nor logical. Assad is not the only player in this game nor a dictator disconnected from any other power. He is connected to the most powerful and well-established intelligence organizations in the world. His regime is an international business. None of the owners of this business are going to leave the security of this empire up to the stupidity of a dumb dictator. So, every action taken was studied and deliberately chosen. But for what purpose?

That is what I will try to explain throughout the following pages of this book.

---

must go" and I said: "Huh, how is he going to do that? Where is the policy for that?" and we know they sent in the CIA to overthrow Assad. The CIA and Saudi Arabia together in covert operations tried to overthrow Assad. It was a disaster. Eventually it brought in both Isis as a splinter group to the jihadists that went in. It also brought in Russia. [...] This is what I would call "the permanent state", this is the CIA, this is the Pentagon. [...] We have made a proxy war in Syria. It has killed 500,000 people, displaced 10 million, and I'll say predictably so, because I predicted it seven years ago, that there was no way to do this, and it would make a complete chaos" Prescribed from MSNBC Panel On Syria, https://www.youtube.com/watch?v=_O2TRzA2ezk

The book contains two kind of materials: Facts and theory.
They are, of course connected to each other.

The facts described in this book I have witnessed personally. However, I tried to provide many outside sources to back them up whenever possible.
There is a dilemma regarding references in our time: readers vary when it comes to the sources they accept. Some accept only western media, other reject everything from these sources. Meeting all variations would just add hundreds of pages to the book which would just fill it with information the average user can access easily in many ways. I don't ask the reader to accept my witness or my sources. I appreciate the skeptical attitude and invite the skeptical reader to investigate any doubted information the way they like. I think in our time, this has become easier. The readers can search, research, even reach neutral Syrians or firsthand witnesses. There are many options available.

The theoretical parts try to explain the facts. More importantly, they were concluded from these facts and built on them. They came later as a result, because the classic explanations were found invalid or insufficient. I would emphasize here **that I am not fan of any previous or popular theory, especially the conspiracy theories**. I can't stand listening to more than a few seconds to any story about the Rothschild family or the Freemasons' power. I used to accept the simple explanation in the stream of media in the first couple of crisis' years (till mid 2013). This explanation describes what happens in Syria as a "freedom revolution against a dictator tries to maintain his power". Or, in the best cases, a "Power conflict between the west and Russia".

At some point, any of these explanations couldn't answer all of the questions. It was possible to skip over them and ignore the paradoxes. Most of the others did this and could live with some story, they found some stream of media that meets their understanding. I tried that as well, but failed. My respect for my mind, for the images of the victims, for the mission of the intellectual, all of that left no chance for me to keep my eyes closed. I had to dig deeper and deeper.

If I ask the reader to investigate any doubted fact, I would ask them even to try to contradict any part of the theory. I would appreciate any contradiction that explains the facts clearly. I have just one condition before doing that: Read all the facts carefully before providing any simplified explanation. I would be thankful to any reader who can provide a more logical explanation, provided that this alternative explanation comes *after* reading the facts carefully.

Was the Assad regime the victim of the Syrian revolution or its creator?

In this chapter I will illustrate in facts what I called in the preface the "mysterious behavior of the Assad regime" during the Syrian crisis. . I will list 10 facts as examples of this ambiguous behavior and describe them briefly.

This behavior was explained by the stream media as merely "stupidity" or "the expected reaction of a dictator trying to maintain his position". Obviously, I don't agree with this.

This part is about FACTS, no theory here. I witnessed these facts first hand and added -when possible- references from various trusted sources. However, I would appreciate if the reader went even further and investigated these facts from other sources they might trust more.

My own theory to explain this behavior will come in a later essay. That explanation is my own. The reader can contradict it. No facts there. However, I will also use several outside sources to support it.

Summer 2011 - Saraqib – North Syria

The weather is too hot. I woke up this morning and turned the TV on. This channel shows movies 24 hours and I watch it to improve my English. I was still not awake from the stupor which covered Saraqib for the last few days.

Just a few days ago, my father came at the same time in the morning, telling me that the army entered the city with tanks and soldiers to implement the arresting campaign and inspection. He was afraid. He took our cash and hid it somewhere in the bathroom. We were not sure if the army might come to the farm area which is 3 Km away from Saraqib's City center. A few hours later, heavy gunfire started nearby. My father got even more scared. Nothing justified such heavy gunfire. There were no weapons or armed people in the whole area. After a few seconds, there was a knock on the door. I dared to go out and invite him to the farm to "honor" us and enter, calling him as usual in Syria at that time "My Sir". While he entered, he asked me about my name, my ID Card and my youngest brother who was very involved in the demonstrations against the regime. After the inspection were done, they left, taking one of our two cars as it was registered in my youngest brother's name, and stealing some other stuff. A few minutes later, my mother called my father asking him to come as another army group was inspecting our house in the city center. When we went there, a third group stopped us and checked our ID cards comparing them to their lists. My father's name was there. They arrested him. We could get him released a few days later along with the car. We paid some bribes and used some connections. He came home stunned, swinging between fear, anger, grudge, and courage.

In this inspection, which was the first of two, nobody was killed. The army arrested some intellectual persons including my father, and released most of them later, after insulting and torturing them.

The movie is still playing. I feel as if I am drugged. I see scenes of inspections in rural areas by heavy vehicles and armed soldiers, I hear words like "minority" and "historical grudge." I see that this minority is becoming armed and hectic. Yet I also see an unarmed, scared majority. They stay tuned to terrifying rumors that something horrible is coming soon. Propaganda channels broadcast with soaring tone and provoking content. International Organizations watch, helpless but aware of what is happening. The majority trusts that the international community is not going to allow massacre, hope for a western intervention that would arrive sometime, maybe at the last moment. It doesn't.

At some point I asked myself, am I watching a film about what happened in Saraqib few days ago? But the men are black and the scenes seem to be in Africa. But the scenario is so fucking similar. Am I still asleep or just raving? Which film is this?
I read the title of the film in the corner "Hotel Rwanda".

Ah, Rwanda? Is that what happened in Rwanda?
And why does that scenario look so similar to our reality?

***

While thousands of foreign fighters were flooding into Syria, the Syrian regime's army was working at full capacity to destroy Syrian cities one by one[5]. This didn't change when the Russian air forces took over part of the destroying operation[6]. The fighters were crossing the Syrian borders on a daily basis, armed with tons of weapons and vehicles. They came mainly from the Turkish borders and partially from Jordan, Lebanon and Iraq. In almost no cases were the fighters' convoys attacked. They were moving in plain sight, without challenge. Neither the Syrian regime's nor the Russians' air forces tried to stop them.

Further, and Soon after the rebellion started, the regime released thousands of arrested radicals who were detained in the famous prisons Sednaya and Palmira[7].

---

[5] https://edition.cnn.com/2017/04/06/middleeast/syria-weapons-against-civilians/index.html

[6] https://www.amnesty.org/en/press-releases/2016/03/syrian-and-russian-forces-targeting-hospitals-as-a-strategy-of-war/

[7] See also Der Spiegel newspaper's report: "Around the beginning of the Syrian uprising, in March 2011, Assad once again released jihadists from the country's prisons. Simultaneously, tens of thousands of Syrian students, liberal activists, and human rights advocates began being arrested. Their fates were recently documented by Human Rights Watch, which alleges that many have been detained arbitrarily, tortured, and subjected to unfair trials." http://www.spiegel.de/international/world/former-prisoners-fight-in-syrian-insurgency-a-927158.html

Also the Telegraph report about the same issue: "Sednaya Prison, northeast of Damascus, Syria. Thousands of political prisoners have been held here by President Assad's regime, and it is well attested that President Bashar al-Assad ran hot and cold on jihadists throughout his reign. He encouraged them to go to Iraq

These prisons were described as "labs for manufacturing the terrorists".

General Khaled Al Mutlak, a defected Syrian officer, wrote in a very informative article:

> *"Sednaya prison has been and still is a labor for the Syrian regime intelligence service agencies. It produces personalities who are against the regime, who are suspected of terrorism and who became, upon their release, the main tools in achieving the goals of the Assad regime. [...] They took command positions of the factions which were described as Islamist, with full support from Arabic and International Intelligence Agencies."*[8]

---

to join Zarqawi's al-Qaeda offshoot, the predecessor to Isil, and fight America after 2003, but also jailed many on their return home if they seemed to pose a similar threat to his own rule. When the uprising in Syria began in spring 2011, he released hundreds of them under an amnesty. The amnesty, supposedly for political prisoners, was denounced at the time as a fraud, or too little too late. In fact, it was one of the most important political acts Mr. Assad made. The prisoners released were mostly Islamists, who went on to join or form a string of armed groups, while secular and peaceful protesters and activists continued to be jailed and killed." http://s.telegraph.co.uk/graphics/projects/isis-jihad-syria-assad-islamic/

[8] https://www.syria.tv/content/مختبرات-ترويض-الإرهاب . Mutlak thinks that "the story of manufacturing and preparing those persons among others started on 2005. The Syrian Intelligence agencies implemented a practical training program to prepare Jihadist Islamists and civilians who have been qualified as a part of a bigger test of internal expected conflict. The place of this test was Sydnaya prison where the prison was gradually handed to the

General Mutlak named some examples of these figures like:

- Abu Lokman, one of the founders of the Al Nusra front in Syria, who also worked as ISIS Leader (Emir) in Al Raqqa [North Syria, and the capital of ISIS in Syria]
- Mahmoud Al Kholaif, the security officer in ISIS
- Haj Fadel Al Agha, the relations officer
- Abu Abdul Rahman Al Hamwi, Al Nusra leader in Hama
- Abu Naser Darwasha, the cousin of Abu Mohammad Al Jawlani, the leader of HTS (Hayat Tahrir Al Sham, previously Al Nusra Front)
- Abu Hafs Al Keswani, the Islamist leader in Daraa, and others.

"'The reason the regime released them at the beginning of the Syrian revolution was to complete the militarization of the uprising,' said Naser, who defected in late 2012. 'And to spur criminal acts so that revolution would become a criminal case and give the impression that the regime is fighting terrorists' [...] John Kerry, the outgoing secretary of state, said in November 2015 that ISIS 'was created by Assad' and by former

---

Islamists prisoners starting from the first intractableness (27 March 2009), then the second one (5 June 2008)".

Iraqi Prime Minister Nouri al-Maliki, both of whom released al Qaeda prisoners in their respective countries. Assad's aim was to tell the world, 'It's me or the terrorists.'"[9]

Most analysts, opposition thinkers and writers agree with this analysis.

My objection to this simple explanation is: the Assad regime achieved this goal within the first two years. There is a big question mark hovering over this. By 2013 Isis occupied large parts of Syria and Iraq. With the news dominating international media and Syrians fed up with the Islamists and foreign factions, the Assad regime had the justification it needed to end the armed rebellion and restore its control over Syria. As I will explain in the following points, the Assad regime did the exact opposite.

The different headquarters of the armed opposition stayed unmolested during the seven years of the militarized rebellion. Armed rebels grew in number in each small town or city center across the area controlled by the opposition. The factions of this opposition, led now by unknown foreigner fighters, occupied government buildings and schools and turned them into military buildings. These headquarters were always surrounded with armed vehicles. They were

---

[9] "Assad Henchman: Here's How We Built ISIS" a two-year investigation by The Daily Beast shows. https://www.thedailybeast.com/assad-henchman-heres-how-we-built-isis

completely visible and could be easily monitored and observed. The Syrian and Russian aircraft were flying over these headquarters on a daily basis while their raids attacked the civilian hospitals, markets, childrens' schools and houses[10]. Neither the Syrian aircraft and later the Russian ones tried to bother the headquarters of the armed opposition. They even avoided causing any harm to them.

In many events, the tanks of the opposition were marching peacefully towards their destination without any attack, or even fear of the attack.

One of the most illustrative examples was when;

> *"An entire 1,000-strong rebel brigade based in Syria's Idlib province has reportedly defected to the Islamic State group [...] The Dawud Brigade, which was based in Sarmin and fell under the umbrella of the anti-government Sham Army, arrived in the northeastern city of Raqqa last weekend, the main headquarters for the Islamic State (IS) – previously known as the Islamic State of Iraq and Syria[11] (ISIS/ISIL). [The distance between*

---

[10] https://edition.cnn.com/2017/04/06/middleeast/syria-weapons-against-civilians/index.html

[11] The exact scene was also seen in the battle of liberating Idlib city center in the north of Syria. The convoys of opposition tanks were marching gloriously towards the City Center under the sun. https://www.youtube.com/watch?v=OQ71KXgNAU4. On that day, the Syrian aircrafts attacked Sarmin city, which is 3 Km away from Idlib. These attacks killed many civilians and caused a lot of damage to the central market, hospitals, and children schools in Sarmin and its countryside! "On March 28, 2015, a coalition of

Sarmin and Raqqa is over 200 Km, plain land, during that time the Syrian airplanes were flying and attacking the civilians not so far[12]] The rebel group arrived in a convoy of over 100 vehicles, including 10 tanks seized from Syrian government forces.[13]

This actually poses two questions, not just one.

First, why were these convoys not bothered by the Russian and Syrian airplanes? In some cases these

---

Islamist rebel groups including Ahrar al-Sham and jihadists from the Al-Nusra Front, now known as Fatah al-Sham Front, seized the Sunni-majority city. [...] Syrian warplanes, and later Russian jets, have repeatedly targeted cities and towns in Idlib province." http://www.dailymail.co.uk/wires/afp/article-4386878/Idlib-Last-Syrian-rebel-stronghold.html

[12] https://www.independent.co.uk/news/world/middle-east/syria-conflict-isis-marches-further-into-syria-tipping-the-balance-of-power-in-the-civil-war-9608335.html
https://www.hrw.org/news/2014/07/30/syria-barrage-barrel-bombs
http://www.dailystar.com.lb/News/Middle-East/2014/Jun-16/260322-twenty-dead-in-syria-barrel-bomb-attack-in-aleppo.ashx

[13] https://www.rt.com/news/171952-thousand-strong-defect-islamic-state/
Read also in the same report: "Brigade's leader [was] Hassan Abound [which is also ex-Sydney prisoner who was freed by the Syrian regime 2011]
"Meanwhile there have been reports on Monday that several rebel factions affiliated with the FSA have pledged allegiance to the IS in the border town of al-Bokmal in eastern Syria. [...] The reports of the defections come as the Obama administration ratchets up efforts to arm the Free Syrian Army. Last month the White House asked Congress for half-a-billion dollars in aid to go towards the opposition fighters."

---

airplanes were attacking hospitals and civilian markets, while flying over these moving tanks.

The second question mark is even bigger: where did this trust and serenity of the opposition tanks came from? Where did they get the assurance that they wouldn't be attacked, so they didn't even try to hide?

In some areas that stayed under the control of the regime like Aleppo and Damascus, the armed opposition was allowed to stay close to the city centers. During the crisis years, these opposition points launched on a daily basis locally made shells to kill a couple of inhabitants. Some of these points were not far from Assad's palace no more than a few kilometers and stayed so for years. Although it was very easy and closer to the heart of the regime to destroy these points, the regime aircraft skipped them and focused on targets hundreds of kilometers away. This guaranteed the loyalty of the inhabitants who were mostly Christian, Druze or belonged to other minorities. This also created a hostile attitude against the opposition. Words like "freedom", "democracy" or "revolution" became the ugliest words these inhabitants could hear.

On the other hand, the Assad's regime was keen to arrest or kill peaceful activists and publicly insult the intellectuals and the elders[14] in many targeted areas.

---

[14] As I promised the reader, I will postpone my own explanation of the events to the next essay, and keep this essay for facts only. However, I would take this opportunity to wonder here if the above described behavior of Assad's regime has anything to do with an exact similar behavior somewhere else in this world,

During the eight year revolution, the arrest of innocents, women, children and peaceful activists didn't stop. They were tortured and degraded[15] in horrible ways. This became a phenomena represented by thousands of cases, many of which were leaked and documented.

In many cases, the arrested or tortured were merely neutral innocents or even pro regime citizens.

Many thinkers explained this behavior of the regime as a tactic to militarize the revolution. According to them, the peaceful revolution was dangerous to the regime and scared it because of the potential for regime collapse. This explanation sounds logical to some extent. However, this behavior of the regime continued

---

namely in Pakistan as James Risen reported in his exceptional book "Pay Any Price":

"On March 17, 2011, American drones fired at least two missiles into a gathering in Data Khel that killed more than forty people. The U.S. government insisted that the drone strike killed a Taliban commander, but villagers later told investigators that drones had attacked a meeting of a local elders gathered to negotiate a dispute over a chromite mine. Many of those killed were men who were both local elders and heads of large families. Their deaths triggered yet another round of anti-American protest in Pakistan." Pay Any Price, James Risen, PP 2015, P 55.

[15] "Forces loyal to Syrian President Bashar al-Assad went on a systematic killing spree, murdering at least 108 people. Most shockingly, the killers targeted women and children. A U.N. representative said the victims included 49 children who were younger than 10. The al-Assad regime denied it carried out the atrocities, but U.N. officials said they saw clear evidence that the Syrian government was involved in the attacks." https://edition.cnn.com/2012/05/31/opinion/ghitis-syria-killing-children/index.html

even after the revolution was deeply militarized, Islamized and even globalized. The regime got enough indications and proof of radical and armed rebellion in the first year of the revolution. That could be enough justification to suppress the rebellion. So why didn't this unjustified brutality stop during the eight years of the revolution?

The regime has been clearly and systematically encouraging the armed movements, while brutally suppressing any peaceful activities.

At the start of the rebellion, the rebels obtained most of their weapons from the Syrian regime itself. The Assad regime's officers sold the rebels everything they needed. This initially appeared as mere corruption. However, anyone who has a basic knowledge of Syrian affairs will know that it is impossible for such a thing to happen without a green light from the central command of the Assad regime's intelligence services. The risk is very high and the discovery of such deals is almost certain. No sane officer would risk so much for a few thousand bucks. This could mean an eternity in hell for the officer, their families and even their clans. After the Hama Massacre in 1982, no Syrian would have had the courage to sell a cigarette to someone fighting against the regime. Even just speaking to some suspected person was a crime, let alone selling weapons. When such deals start to take place on a regular basis, under similar conditions across the whole country, that cannot be accidental. This is a systematic process, with full consent from the high central command of the Assad regime's intelligence agencies[16]. Most of these officers who committed such deals moved to areas controlled by the regime, where they would live for many years. None of them were investigated or punished for these deals.

Soon after the demonstrations started (or even before), some so-called "leaked videos" started to spread in the social media or were broadcast on a daily basis on international TV news channels. These videos were leaked from Assad's military points, prisons or officials. They were full of all the things that provoke people: insulting their holy stuff, torturing, insulting their honor (women), in short, everything that makes Syrians (and radical Muslims all around the world) to go crazy, thus, leaving them no chance but to rebel. For those radicals around the world, their only option was to travel to Syria to "respond to the Jihad call or to protect their sister Muslimas' honor".

The important point here is: leaking such videos or even photos used to be completely impossible for 40 years! As I said, the criminality of the Assad regime didn't start in 2011, and the most brutal practices were happening in Syria during the four decades and across the 14 regions on a daily basis, but none of these

---

[16] In one of the inspection campaign processed by Assad Regime against Saraqib, my town, the soldiers caught an armed leader from the opposition. The soldiers called the high command happily to inform them of the siege. The brutal furious answer came from their command: Release him, you bastards.

practices had the chances to be leaked under any circumstance. The Syrians and Assad officers know that whoever leaked information against the government's will, will be soon and definitely known and punished like hell, along with his relatives and beloved people. Although the regime media pretended publicly to be pissed off with such videos and denied them, a simple checking of these "leaked" videos shows that they were recorded freely by easy-to-know recorders (not by scared ones or by using hidden or fixed cameras for instance), and they were recorded and spread systematically on a daily basis during the crisis.

Assad didn't use his full power and arsenal when the rebellion started. On the contrary, he deliberately intended to send signals of his weakness to the rebels to encourage them to go ahead. Militarily, he used very classic reactions and used a very soft tone and assured the claims of his "supposed enemies and conspirers" that he is really scared and his regime was really about to fall down in a matter of days! (The media worked hard to convince the Syrians with this fact until it became undoubted).

Using bomb barrels and missiles started only when it became too late to turn back or to quit the rebellion or even to think about making a deal with the regime.
It became too late to turn back when:
- The foreign fighters became the strongest power on the ground, established their arsenals and armed headquarters, and somehow became

disconnected from the locals, treating them arrogantly or ignorantly.

- On the other hand, the Syrians who were prepared to adopt the attitude of "going ahead for freedom and dignity until death" didn't have this obligation when the rebellion started. The Assad regime used its full power only when they committed and withdrawing became very humiliating for them. In this time, the media channels, mainly Al Jazeera kept praising those sacrificing their lives for freedom and terrorizing any tendency to make peace or agreement with the regime, considering even thinking about that as a betrayal of the martyrs' blood and the freedom's principles. Turning back also became impossible for Syrians who obey their commitments, no matter how much they lose, and regardless of what the tragedy they suffer are (especially after they have been prepared for that in many ways as I will explain in other parts of this book).

The Army and regime forces adopted multiple standards behavior across the country. Some areas were meant to be kept out of the opposition's grip. Others were meant to go in this grip very early and stay there. Between these two poles there were other shadows. Some areas were meant to be given to the opposition for a while then restored again by the regime. These were decided based upon each area's ethnicity, religion, sect, or living standards[17]. In the areas which were intended to stay pro-Assad, the regime forces were instructed to behave like angels. In the other parts, the regime's "devil" forces were sent there to drive the people mad.

Years before the revolution started, some figures belonging to the Assad's family clan (like Rami Makhlouf, Bashar Al Assad's cousin) were enlarged through propaganda as corruption symbols. They were given the main economy sectors like the communication sector, media, luxury hotels and free zone areas (one person owned these whole sectors (among others)!). Assad's corrupted regime didn't actually need this "statue" to acquire or steal the Syrians' wealth; it used to be corrupted during three decades of the father's era without such phenomena which was not really necessary. It was not difficult for a regime with such educated leader to keep the corruption hidden as in his father's time (if the financial profit was the goal). But what happened is exactly the opposite: this phenomenon was enlarged through widely spread propaganda (led by the Syrian intelligence agencies themselves). The smart leader didn't stop or reduce this phenomenon, rather, he

---

[17] Areas like big city centers, rich neighborhoods, Christian, Alawites, and Druze were treated completely different from countryside areas which were pushed or even tempted to go ahead in the rebellion process.

strengthened it throughout the years before the revolution and after. This was used to give the crowds enough reason to start the rebellion. The first motto used in the 2011 demonstrations was exactly against the corruption of this "MADE" symbol.

CONCLUSION:

What I tried to prove through the previous 10 facts, is that Assad was not simply "that corrupted regime which was afraid of revolution and worked hard to avoid it, and then started to kill people widely and brutally when it erupted", as the stream media would like to explain.

The Assad regime <u>deliberately</u> intended to create this "revolution" and triggered it. He strived to give this revolution everything it needed to start and worked hard to keep it alive when it was about to burn out, all with full coordination and collaboration with his supposed enemies i.e. Turkey and its axis countries, as I will describe in the following chapter.

However, after 8 years of all kinds of predictions and analyses, it seems that Assad was not behaving randomly. Those, who either consulted or instructed him were aware of their goal. Assad is still in his palace on the top of his regime which slowly restored its internal and international position. His clan and officers have doubled their wealth. He rid himself of half of his nations which he considered "unnecessary" elements.

The countries which acted as if they were interested in toppling him were not really serious about that. As I will illustrate in the following chapters, they helped the beginning of the rebellion but strived to hinder what most of the Syrians hoped for, i.e. toppling Assad and building a democratic state. While the stream media explained thousands of mistakes and amateur behaviors of countries like United States, France,

Great Britain, and countries instructed directly by these countries. (Turkey, Saudi Arabia, Qatar and so on.) While the media believed that the politicians and intelligence agencies of these countries were just amateurs and confused, I personally was not in the mood to believe that. I am just not prepared mentally to take such jokes seriously, especially when it has to do with millions of victims and human disasters.

In his valuable book "Destroying a Nation: The Civil War in Syria", Ambassador Nikolaos Van Dam pose this question: "Could the war in Syria have been avoided?"
He sees that:

> *"if the opposition forces had not been supported in the way they were, the revolution might possibly have been suppressed earlier with fewer victims, and the regime might have continued its repressive rule for another indefinite period."*

This is exactly what happened in countries like Egypt. In Egypt, the demonstrations could even topple the regime, which was able to maneuver and recovered quickly.
I am not trying to express an appreciation to the maneuvers and recovery of totalitarian regimes. There are 2 cases in which I wouldn't write this book: If the countries which supported the Syrian opposition went to the last step, i.e. toppling the regime, or if they didn't support the opposition in the first place, leaving the Egyptian scenario to take its natural place in Syria.

What the west and Turkey did was eliminating this option. Their role was devoted to guaranteeing that the revolution spread in the Syrian body to the extent that removing the revolution means amputating the whole body. What happened in Syria is exactly what the Ambassador chose for his book title "destroying a nation".

Van Dam thinks, if a scenario like the Egyptian on has happened in the Syrian case, that:

> *"some day, in the future, there was bound to be renewed effort by those people who had suffered from atrocities of al-Asad regime to have a violent reckoning".*

Egypt lost some of its courageous sons, whose number is estimated, in the worst case as less than 0.0001% of its population. The economy suffered a bit, then all was recovered. If the story ended or there would be other upcoming episodes, that is another discussion.
The majority of Syrians wouldn't regret paying their lives with pleasure as a price to enter history gloriously as a nation that achieved its freedom with its blood. This was their ambition, part of their dignity and their self-esteem - that was their goal. Further, a heavy media wave before and during the revolution prepared them for that as I will explain later.
The catastrophic part of the story: the price was paid, but the glorious freedom didn't come. The Syrians lost their nation, but they didn't rid of the regime.

The dialogue about difference between the Egyptian and Syrian cases is not about a film we watched and sat in a luxurious cafeteria to wish it was written or directed other way. The difference is counted with millions of human victims, "predictably so because I predicted it seven years ago, that there was no way to do this, and it would make a complete chaos" so Jeffrey Sachs, director of the Earth Institute at Columbia University.

These was not merely a mistake nor could it be explained as an estimation error. The intelligence forces which managed this operation were, simply put, the most sophisticated intelligence organizations in the world- namely the CIA, jointly cooperating with French, British and of course Turkish, Saudi and other organizations.

Instead of leading these bodies to work on toppling the larger regime, they directed them to smaller bodies. They turned their back to the regime, which in turn ignored them. Both the regimes and these bodies worked on turning the lives of Syrians into hell. This continued until these groups left the areas they occupied back to Turkey, handing these areas to the regime with so-called: "peace agreements". These were just stage plays, exactly like the battles in which they fought against the regime. The regime gave each of these groups the chance to gain temporary victory. These groups had destroyed the rebellion and gave the regime more popularity. Everything else for the regime that was lost is marginal and can be recovered.

"Donor countries (like United States and Turkey) sometimes simultaneously gave contradictory instructions to Syrian military commanders in battles with the Islamic State, threatening to stop their military aid if their instructions were not followed up. Syrian commanders also complained about the lack of relevant military intelligence, which could have been provided in time by their foreign supporters, and about lack of sufficient ammunition (which they occasionally described as a kind of "drip-feeding"). Opposition commanders sometimes felt betrayed."

"Western criticism of the military opposition, concerning a lack of coordination, was therefore unjustified insofar as this was a result of a lack of Western military coordination"[18].

---

[18] Destroying a Nation: The Civil War in Syria, by Nikolaos Van Dam, pp 2018.

Masters of Syria

Syria got its independence from the ending of the French Mandate in 17 April 1946. In the aftermath the young independent country witnessed series of military coups.

The first military coup in modern Syrian history was led by the Syrian Army chief of staff, Husni al-Za'im. It overthrew the country's democratically elected government. This coup was engineered by the CIA.

Hashim al-Atassi came to power in 1949 by a coup led by Sami al-Hinnawi who acted as president for one day. It took one year before another coup led by Adib ShishaklI took the power from Al Atassi.

In February 1954 another coup overthrew the government of Adib ShishaklI after he stayed in power for one day.

Syria became the northern region in the United Arab Republic, which unified Egypt and Syria in 1958. In 1961, one more coup broke up the united republic and restored an independent Syrian Republic.

The 1963 coup brought the Ba'ath Party to the power. It is referred to as "the 8 March Revolution" by the Syrian government and was inspired by a similar Iraqi military coup. There were a lot of reports and evidences which proved the involvement of the American Agencies and the Soviet Union in enabling the Iraqi coup which inspired its Syrian counterpart.

The 1966 coup came after events between 21 and 23 February ended with the replacement of the government of the Syrian Arab Republic. The National

Command of the Ba'ath Party was removed from power by the party's Military Committee and its Regional Command.

> *"Governing Syria has never been easy, as the commanders of punitive expeditions from Titus to the Ottomans' last general could attest. Two years into the French League of Nations Mandate over Syria and Lebanon, a Scottish traveler, Helen Cameron Gordon, toured the country and later described conditions that would daunt any sovereign, foreign or local. She wrote:*
>
> *"Her inhabitants are made up of at least dozen different races, mainly Asiatic, and worse still, of about thirty religious sects, all suspicious and jealous of each other.*
>
> *Sir Mark Sykes, in his Dar Ul-Islam: A Record of a Journey through Ten of the Asiatic Provinces of Turkey (1904), similarly observed:*
>
> *The population of Syria is so inharmonious a gathering of widely different races in blood, in creed, and in custom, that government is both difficult and dangerous."[19]*

Hafez al-Assad's coup on 13 November 1970 was the last coup in Syria. he called it "The Corrective Movement".

---

[19] Charles Glass, Syria Burning: A Short History of a Catastrophe. ISBN-13: 978-1784785161

Hafez Al Assad's coup was not a unique case, in which a coup seizes the power for decades after several previous coups. Many countries witnessed this exact scene, like Iraq, Libya, Venezuela, Algeria, North Korea etc..

This poses a few questions: How could these military governors monopolize the power all these decades? Did they use special techniques to end the frequent coups phenomena?

How can we explain that they did that almost in the same era? Did they just learn from each other or were there some superior entities supporting them with unified recipes?

According to the Newsweek:

> *"After Nasser's defeat of the region's old colonial masters—Britain and France—in the 1956 Suez Crisis, Russian arms and money began pouring into the region. Soviet engineers dammed the Nile at Aswan, and helped construct modern cities in Baath Party-run Syria and Iraq. At the same time, an entire generation of Arab officers, doctors and professionals studied in Moscow—including future Egyptian President Hosni Mubarak and Haftar, who received training in the Soviet Union in the 1970s after graduating from Benghazi Military Academy. KGB generals helped build the security services of Libya, Algeria, Egypt, Iraq and Syria in the image of*

the Soviet secret police. Anxious to stop the Communist domino effect in the Middle East, Washington threw money at the problem. Israel, Saudi Arabia and Egypt—after Nasser's fall—became major recipients of U.S. military aid. Turkey, a NATO member since 1952, hosted American planes, warships and, most controversially, Jupiter medium-range missiles. [...]Moscow's key ally was Palestinian leader Mahmoud Abbas, who earned a doctorate at the Peoples' Friendship University in Moscow in the 1970s. Israeli researchers, citing documents that KGB archivist Vasili Mitrokhin smuggled out of Russia in 1991, have claimed that Abbas was recruited by the Soviet security service under the code name "Krotov"—although Palestinian officials dismissed the allegation as an Israeli smear. Agent or not, Abbas "likes the Russians, he wants to please them," says Ziad Abu Zayyad, a former Palestinian minister and negotiator. [...]One by one, Moscow's clients began to fall. Iraq's Saddam Hussein—who had at times received U.S. support—was the first to go. [...] Cairo has long been a key military, intelligence and diplomatic partner for Washington. As the recipient of the second-largest amount of U.S. military aid, Egypt continued this partnership even when relations with Obama strained following Sisi's power grab in 2013. While close ties with Washington have been *maintained since then, Egypt has also acknowledged Moscow's new-found status by hosting an air drill for Russia last year—the Kremlin's first such exercise in Africa. Last November, Egypt also signaled its support for Putin by becoming one of only four countries to support Russia's resolution on Syria in the United Nations. Moscow, in turn, has pushed to lift U.N. sanctions on Libya, where Haftar, Sisi's ally, is still vying to become the country's military strongman. "Putin will undertake to revoke [sanctions]," Haftar told reporters after his video conference in January with Shoigu on Russia's aircraft carrier."*[20]

Assad's family –for instance- belongs to a minority sect which used to be highly discriminated against throughout their history. The Syria community is a complicated one, which contains a lot of contradicting sects, tribes and clans. In a country like Syria, where people are very racist, a family like the Assad family has no chance to govern the Syrians in a semi-royal way for decades without very intelligent techniques.

In my opinion, these leaders and families stayed in power could not do such a job alone. No matter how charismatic these leaders or how smart they were, Muammar Al Qaddafi, Hafiz Al Assad or Saddam Houssine, Fidel Castro or Hugo Chavez and others

---

[20]   http://newsweek.com/how-russia-became-middle-easts-new-power-broker-554227

could not do such a complicated job of controlling nations in a semi-royal way without external help.

The danger in such a situation comes from the fact that the president becomes completely dependent upon the entities which train, qualify and update the capabilities of his services and directorates. The power of the president relies merely on the organizational capabilities of these entities which are created and updated by a foreign power. The president's chance to say "no" to any instruction that comes from his "Godfather" is almost zero. Qualifying the capabilities of the security services is constant work and not a one-time job. It always needs to update according to the local and global developments and non-stop overseeing of all kind of updates.

However, if the sponsor has pledged to protect the president and keep his family in power or prosperity, why would such a family say "no" or even think about it, no matter how crazy the instructions actually could be?

The Assad's Recipe to staying in Power

In this chapter, I will describe some techniques that the Assad regime used to minimize the possibilities of any coup that could take him out of power and guaranteed that the Assad's family govern Syria in a semi-Royal way for decades.

Multiplying the security services agencies

Hafez Al Assad (the father of Bashar) had many security service agencies. He inherited some from past regimes, and created others. His main 4 security directorates were:

- The General Intelligence Directorate (Amn Addawlah) was formed few months after Hafiz Al Assad came to power.
- The military intelligence service of Syria (Al-Mukhabarat al-'Askariyya) was established in 1969. Hafez Al Assad was the minister of Defense at the time. Its roots go back to the French mandate period (1923–1943)[21].
- *"The Political Security Directorate (Idarat al-Amn al-Siyasi) conducts surveillance within the country, looking for signs of opposition political activity. Its role overlaps to some*

---

[21] Hizbollah–Syrian Intelligence Affairs: A Marriage of Convenience, a study by Carl Anthony Wege, College of Coastal Georgia
http://scholarcommons.usf.edu/cgi/viewcontent.cgi?article=1097&context=jss

extent that of the General Security (or Intelligence) Directorate (Idarat al-Amn al-'Amm), the principal civilian intelligence agency in the country. The latter also has an external security division equivalent to the U.S. Central Intelligence Agency, as well as a Palestine division, which oversees activities of Palestinian groups in Syria and Lebanon."

- *The fourth intelligence service, the Air Force Intelligence Directorate (Idarat al-Mukhabarat al-Jawiyya) is only nominally tied to the air force. Its role as the most powerful and feared intelligence agency in Syria comes from the fact that Hafez al-Assad was once air force commander, and later turned the air force intelligence service into his personal action bureau. In addition to intelligence work, the directorate has assisted numerous terrorist operations abroad."[22]*

Each of the above directorates has a branch in every one of the 14 Syrian provinces, besides several platoons in big cities.

It is expected that there is a sort of distribution of roles between these directorates, but this is not the situation. Each of these services was given unrestricted power to oversee and report everything that was happening. For instance, the role of "Palestine division" was not really

---

[22] http://www.faqs.org/espionage/Sp-Te/Syria-Intelligence-and-Security.html

overseeing "activities of Palestinian groups in Syria and Lebanon ". It has been known as the most brutal division that tortured thousands of Syrians who were not necessarily connected to Palestine nor to Lebanon. In my opinion, the aim of creating multiple divisions was to make these services observers of not only the activities of any potential threaten of the regime's power, but rather to oversee each other as well.

Every general or director of these directorates could be a victim of reports written by a small spy in another directorate. With this technique, the Assad regime could minimize the possibility of any potential coup or rebellion. It created horrifying directorates which terrorized the citizens. However, these "terrorizers" were themselves terrorized by the ghosts of their counterparts and colleagues.

The above-described directorates were the secret police. There was the regular police directorate which was responsible for the regular issues and enjoyed much less power than the secret police. Other secret police divisions were added in Bashar Al Assad's era like the Anti-terrorism division or Anti-drugs division. Again, they were just a replication of the main directorates with different names but the same function.

Breakthrough the potential opposition:

This is the other tactic which modern security services developed to complete their control over the nations. It is and advanced technique and one step further. It implies not just overseeing and waiting until the opposition arises, rather, the security services predict this raise and break through any "potential" movement in their very early stages. In each potential rebellion there should be insider agents, and, in some cases, these agents even play the main role in starting the rebellion itself. This is a very advanced tactic but very smart as well. During the Syrian revolution's years, thousands of such double-agents were discovered. Some of them were the main triggers and leaders of the rebellion.

In some advanced stage of this process, the services started to create some factions and movements in parallel with the natural ones and give them power or legitimacy. I mentioned some examples and will mention others throughout the book. Important here: These "Trojan horses" don't necessarily need to be aware of this game. They play their role naturally. The services gave them possibilities in many ways. They trigger the media to create some Aurora and noise around them. It prevents their competitor appearing by assassinating them, arresting them or using any other tools. The modern strategy is: There will always be opposition and we can't prevent that. Let's then create some opposition to keep it other control, while minimizing the influence of any other opposition which we have less control over.

This is a common method which is applied by almost all international intelligence agencies. Throughout this book I mentioned many examples of this technique, applied by United States, the Syrian regime, Iraqi regime and others...

Minds Control

The third technique which guaranteed the exceptional position of Assad's family was mind control. I will not go through this as it needs another book to describe it. However, reading George Orwell's 1984 could describe the scene to a large extent. There were not "telescreens", but the Syrians had the impression that they did exist. There was a popular saying which said "Don't speak, walls have ears".

The Syrian regime controlled all media sources. In Hafez Al Assad's era there were 3 main newspapers belonging exclusively to the government and Al Baath Party. They were directed by the intelligence services. Photos of the "Big Brother" and his inspired sayings were everywhere: on walls, on the first page of every single publication, even children's school books.

Praising the "Correction Movement" was inserted in each curriculum, including 3rd grade biology books . During the first 2 decades of Assad's power, the Syrians had one single TV channel which broadcasted 12 hours a day. Later, another one in the English language would be launched, which broadcasted around 6 hours a day. Until the end of the last century, the Syrians barely had any other source of visual media or news. Assad's exclusive channels broadcasted only the materials which praised "Big Brother" the government's one-sided view. The Soviet fingerprints were clear in creating such a media control system in the exact way that it was created in sister countries like Iraq, Libya, Algeria and so on.

The extreme brutal events of Hama 1982 guaranteed the necessary fear to keep the Syrians away from any oppositional thinking. Using quick and intensified brutality secured afraid and reluctant nations from any political activity against the government. They also were keen to teach their children from their early childhood to "love the homeland and its Master, the Big Brother". Abstaining from that could mean losing these children in unknown places, where "they wish to die, but can't".

No matter how much the exact causalities of the events of the '80s, or what exactly happened there, the rumors that the Syrians believed were enough to domesticate them for decades with no troubles.

The international weakness during the Syrian existence in Lebanon renewed the Syrians' conviction. It assured them that the whole world was complying with their dictator. Some of the Syrians started to link this power with divine powers and became convinced that Assad was just a Frankenstein Monster which couldn't be defeated or toppled.

By the time the Internet and satellite receivers came to life it was too late. The Assad already achieved a full generation of a brainwashed nation. Even when part of the nation started to be informed and enlightened, the majority of the nation stayed loyal to the "Big Brother" and his inspired family. However, there was an increasing feeling that things couldn't stay like this for long. Some action should have to be taken to compensate for the loss of control over the nation.

When you try to read the political landscape of a foreign country, you have to learn – besides the words- the direction of writing. Some nations write from right to left. Others write from top to bottom. If you learn the meanings of words while insisting on reading from left to right, you would almost understand nothing.

When somebody asks me questions like: "Is Assad's regime secular or Islamist?" or "How much did Assad get in the last elections?", I answer: "You know what, you don't need to know the right answer. The question itself is wrong".

The Syrian Playground

The players, the winners and the losers

In the incident that Foreign Policy called "the biggest corruption scandal in modern history" [23]

> *"$4.5 million was found at the residence of Suleyman Aslan, the director of [Turkish] state-owned Halkbank, and $750,000 at the home of Baris Guler, son of the former minister of the interior.*

> *All of the 52 people detained that day were connected in various ways with the ruling Justice and Development Party (AKP). Prosecutors accused 14 people — including Aslan, Zarrab, and several family members of cabinet ministers — of bribery, corruption, fraud, money laundering, and gold smuggling. The whistleblowers who tipped off the police claimed that the son [or two sons[24]] of then-Prime Minister (now President) Recep Tayyip Erdogan was next in line. A firestorm was sparked by the release on YouTube of audio recordings in which Erdogan was reportedly heard telling his son, Bilal, to urgently get rid of tens of millions of dollars. Erdogan has claimed the recordings were a montage but the experts begged to differ. [...]In the course of*

---

[23] https://foreignpolicy.com/2015/01/06/why-turkeys-mother-of-all-corruption-scandals-refuses-to-go-away/

[24] http://haber.sol.org.tr/devlet-ve-siyaset/erdogan-oglunu-koruyor-sorusturma-savcidan-alindi-haberi-84919

the investigation the police confiscated some $17.5 million in cash, money allegedly used for bribery"

"Here's how it worked: The Turks exported some $13 billion of gold to Tehran directly, or through the UAE, between March 2012 and July 2013. In return, the Turks received Iranian natural gas and oil."[25]

"Prosecutor fired on Thursday alleges that police failed to carry out some arrests, including that of a Saudi businessman named Yusuf Al Qadi who is linked to al-Qaeda and has access to high level security officials."[26]

"Al-Qaeda-linked Yusuf Al Qadi and Osama Khoutub, who are among the suspects in a major graft probe, have reportedly fled Turkey after the Justice and Development Party (AK Party) blocked a police raid on Wednesday as İstanbul police refused to comply with orders of prosecutors to detain several suspects in the second leg of the investigation. [...] Saudi businessman Al Qadi's assets were frozen in Turkey after he was named a financer of

---

[25] https://foreignpolicy.com/2013/12/26/irans-turkish-gold-rush/
[26] https://www.businessinsider.com/recap-of-corruption-scandal-in-turkey-2013-12?IR=T
http://www.todayszaman.com/news-335038-report-al-qaeda-suspects-flee-after-turkish-govt-blocks-raid.html

---

terrorism in the international community. News reports point out that the al-Qaeda suspect is allowed to enter Turkey freely and has access to high-level diplomats and security officials, including Undersecretary of the National Intelligence Organization (MİT) Hakan Fidan."[27]

The interesting part of this story is that at that time, Arabic media barely covered this issue. Almost no Arabic media followers knew about it. Even Western media covered it much more shyly compared to similar issues when it comes to Erdogan.

At that time, Arabic media were busy promoting Erdogan as the "inspired leader of the Islamic World," and the "Lion of the Sunnis," who defend the rights of Muslims all over the world and would restore the glory of the Sunni Muslim's Caliphate for which they have been nostalgic for ages.

Even media outlets that support Assad– largely avoided covering this issue, although they usually seek any excuse to attack Erdogan. They fabricate controversies when they don't find any. These media outlets consider the Syrian revolution to be a conspiracy against the Assad regime, with Turkey as the main leader of this conspiracy. The reason for the avoidance of even mentioning this scandal is that Iran is considered the mother of Assad's regime and its

---

[27] http://www.todayszaman.com/news-335038-report-al-qaeda-suspects-flee-after-turkish-govt-blocks-raid.html
http://www.silviacattori.net/spip.php?article5219

main sponsor and supporter. The relationship between Iran and Assad's regime is deep and old, and backed with strong economic, historical and even sectarian considerations.

It took years before the presidents of Turkey, Iran, and Russia started to meet in public. During the first 5 years of the Syrian crisis, they acted as enemies and the media played its part to emphasize this fiction. However, this scandal has revealed what was going on behind the scenes.

How The Turkish regime created the Syrian Crisis

Although the media rarely mentions Turkey while speaking about the Syrian crisis, except as an "innocent neutral neighboring country" and one of the "war victims," the Syrian crisis is actually all about Turkey: No Turkey = no crisis = no ISIS = no war!

> *"Turkey is not the only enabler of the Islamist fundamentalists who have kidnapped and murdered Syrians, Iraqis and Westerners since 2011. Two other Middle East allies of United States and Britain, namely Qatar and Saudi Arabia, funded the groups that became ISIS."[28]*

---

[28] Syria Burning: A Short History of a Catastrophe, Charles Glass, ISBN: 978-1784785161. Read also: *"American Vice President Joe Biden admitted as much to Harvard University's John F. Kennedy Forum:'And what my constant cry was that our biggest problem is our allies - our allies in the region where our largest problem in Syria. The Turks were great friends - and I have the greatest relationship with [Turkish President Recep Tayyip] Erdogan., which I just spent a lot of time with - the Saudis, the Emiratis etc... What were they doing?They were determined to take down Assad and essentially have a proxy Sunni-Shia war, what did they do? They poured hundreds of millions of dollars and tens, thousands of tons into anyone who would fight against the Assad except that the people who were being supplied were al-Nusra and al Qaeda and extremist elements of jihadists coming from other part of the world.'. What Biden neglected to say was*

From the first day of the crisis, Turkish behavior and the Syrian military's behavior were in parallel; the unjustified extreme brutal behaviors occurred in parallel with opening the borders to weapons, fighters and organizing the financial aid from the Arabic Gulf countries.

<u>In mysterious full coordination with the Assad regime</u>, Turkey created the Syrian crisis and has managed it right up to now:

- First, it encouraged the crisis by sending clear messages to the Syrians (mainly to the Sunni majority) to go ahead in their revolution, promising clearly and systematically that Turkey would not let them down or neglect to help them as Muslims, Sunni "brothers" and freedom seekers!

---

that America's allies conducted that policy with the knowledge of the United States, which did nothing to stop it. The weapons supplied to the fanatics were manufactured in the US, and American intelligence in Turkey knew which rebels Turkey, Qatar and Saudi Arabia were assisting. Moreover, the moving forces within ISIS, including its mercurial leader Abu Bakr al-Baghdadi, were graduates of the American prison system in Iraq, where previously non-political Sunni Muslims became radicals."
(This last line reminds us of the Assad's prison Sednaya, and what we described about its prisoners and their roles after releasing them by Assad in the beginning of the revolutions. The international intelligence uses the unified tools and techniques which developed collectively across decades).

- Then the borders were opened systematically for fighters from all around the world, with unlimited amounts of weapons, secret financing from the global black market in order to support certain factions controlled remotely and directed only towards secret precise purposes. The Turkish regime has also been facilitating the rise of ISIS, opening the borders and neglecting any kind of control on human or logistic movements, which guaranteed the launch, survival and growth of the Islamic State (and still does).
- Tight filtering of the help and aid, allowing generously those which complicate the situation and worsen it, while boycotting any help or weapons which could end the crisis or lead to dropping the tyranny (like anti-airplane or any effective weapon that can make difference in the fighting for the sake of opposition, in another word, the weapons which were allowed were only those which helped to START the war, but not those which could END it. These were strictly controlled and prohibited)[29].

---

[29] All kind of heavy vehicles, finance and weapons were allowed to go both sides in-out, while anti-airplane munitions were extremely observed and prohibited. The armed fighters which stayed loyal to the instructions were controlled and prevented from attacking Assad except according to a planned schedule. This led in turn to years of crisis and failure of toppling the regime.

By playing this game, the Turkish Regime seems to achieve huge profits on many respects, which enabled him literally to kidnap 23 million Syrians, extort them and negotiate the world about them, while meanwhile profiting from unlimited sources mainly by:

- Monopolizing the trade of northern Syria, including the movement of the commerce, financial transactions or even human aid.

  "Currency dealers in Turkish cities that border Syria say IS has been moving large sums of money out of its caliphate since early last year. The money flows through the hawala system, an informal web of money-transfer offices that is cheap, fast and almost impossible to regulate. The network of hawala shops in Syria and Turkey has expanded since the start of the Syrian war, allowing refugees, weapons-dealers, oil-smugglers and rebel groups to move cash in and out of the country"[30]

- Blocking the borders, so that the Syrians in true need must pay large bribes[31] to the Turkish

---

[30] https://www.economist.com/middle-east-and-africa/2018/02/22/islamic-state-has-been-stashing-millions-of-dollars-in-iraq-and-abroad

[31] Up to couple of thousands of US dollars per person to enter, and almost double of this amount to be able to leave to Europe. No refund in case they were caught somewhere or couldn't reach! At the time of writing these lines, some Syrians who reside in Europe were paying up to 20,000 US$ for promised unguaranteed visas

Police Mafia to enter Turkey on their way to Europe or the rest of the world.

- Employing and training mercenaries to remove systematically the Syrian assets: factories, facilities, etc. and later monopolizing the trade of these stolen assets including **Syrian monuments. Even the human organs** of the Syrians did not remain out of reach of the Turkish Mafia's control. And later welcoming and hosting these mercenaries with their huge wealth in accounts in the Turkish banks).

"The Syrian Observatory for Human Rights monitored the continuation of individual raids by factions or members of the "Olive Branch" Operation Forces who are led by the Turkish forces, in addition to collecting royalties from citizens through imposing sums of money on farmers and traders, as well as collecting funds from civilians when they raid their homes by robbing their money and jewelry if they found any, and stopping buses on the main and sub roads in Afrin area which lead from it to areas in Idlib and the western and northern countryside of Aleppo, and imposing royalties on passengers and preventing them from completing their way without paying money, also the money is being collected through

---

to Turkey in order to reach their homeland, as they don't dare to go through the Assad regime's way.

imposing a ransom on people in exchange for releasing their children from their jails. "[32]

- Exclusively welcoming rich Syrians and allowing them to live with doubled or tripled costs on the rent or residency, with increasing daily extortion procedures (increasing residency fees, taxes, etc.).
- Profiting from the aid coming from international organization aids, Arab rich countries and the Syrians in Diaspora, which end up in the Turkish banks, contractors and other economy sectors.
- Last but not least, using the Syrians as part of its Troy game, threatening Europe shamelessly of opening the borders for refugees if European Union didn't accept Turkey as a member!, while promising effective locking in case they joined them, extorting Europeans to accept what they really didn't want and used to refuse for ages.

[32] http://www.syriahr.com/en/?p=100887

Behind the Scene: The coordinated and harmonized Roles of the Russian and Turkish Regimes in Creating the Syrian Crisis

"The Kremlin's unlikely new best friend is Turkey, a NATO member and centuries-old foe of Russia"[33]

In the previous Essays, I illustrated many indications of the harmonized actions between the Turkish actions and the reactions of Assad's regime and later the Russian armed forces in Syria. Russia and Assad's forces didn't bother any fighters or weapon convoys fleeing from the Turkish borders into Syria.

From the beginning of the Syrian crisis there was dialogue between Russia and Turkey. It was like a "death dance" with the dancers pretending to approach and try to kill each other. The closer they seemed to killing each other, the more "harmonious" these dancers actually were.

In one of its manifestations, the Syrian crisis in 2011 was nothing but a replication of previous scenarios in modern history. Russia instructed Assad's forces to reproduce a situation similar to the Chechen Wars or an enlarged replication of the '80s crisis in Syria. Russia used these experiments as "case studies", considering them "success stories" which enabled

---

[33] . http://newsweek.com/how-russia-became-middle-easts-new-power-broker-554227

them to control nations for decades without any tangible resistance. The success of these experiments wouldn't remain inside the region. The result would be invested to control and domesticate other nations who would pledge not to commit suicide "like those poor Syrians did!"

To reach this result, all Russia needed was to get rid of its old weapons in the so-called "campaign in Syria".

> *"$ 4 Million is the daily cost of Russia's bombing campaign in Syria".[34]*

This so-called "campaign" was implemented using classic arsenal. It was about randomly dropping thousands of TNT barrels from expired airplanes.

The mafias of Russian and Turkish regimes received the lion's share of the benefits of the Syrian war. This consisted of hundreds of billions of dollars. Using some political and taxation tricks, this money would end in the bank accounts of the governing mafias and their mercenaries.

This game was not a fad: 10 years before that, the Syrian regime played the exact same role with Iraq during the war in 2003.

> *"Ironically, Assad is no stranger to cooperation with radical Islamists, and many jihadists who were held at Sednaya were actually encouraged by the Syrian regime to*

---

[34] Ibid.

undertake campaigns for Islam in the past. In 2003, Syrian intelligence agents lured young men into neighboring Iraq to make life difficult for the Americans there. [35]

The Syrian regime opened the borders to the weapons and Jihadists from Syria and the whole world while welcoming the refugees with their private wealth, capital, or monuments and money which were stolen from the government or individuals. Members of Assad's clan took care of some big deals which transferred the wealth of Saddam Hussein's family to Lebanese banks. Meanwhile, many taxation-legislating changes secured the profits that Syrian individuals achieved from business with refugees to flow into the public treasury, which meant it flowed into the pockets and accounts of the corrupted Assad's officers and mercenaries.

The Syrian war is not a disconnected piece of history; it is simply a continuation of similar cases from the past, either previous wars like in Iraq or Afghanistan, or upcoming ones, possibly in Turkey or other parts of this world. The scenario and tools to create such wars and profit from them are the same with little adaptation according to each case's circumstances.

---

[35]   http://www.spiegel.de/international/world/former-prisoners-fight-in-syrian-insurgency-a-927158.html :

The puzzling role of Qatar and other GCC States

The Qatari role in the Syrian crisis is one of the most puzzling ones. I understand the profits that countries like Turkey or Russia achieved by intervening in Syria. Other countries like the United States, France or Great Britain have a long history of intelligence work and carry a colonializing mentality. Their intervention could also be understood. The role of Qatar and other Arab Gulf states stays very puzzling and not completely understood.

"Doha's leaders were particularly emboldened by the revolt in Libya, where Qatar had played the lead Arab role in the Nato-led intervention."

"Whether in terms of armaments or financial support for dissidents, diplomatic manoeuvring or lobbying, Qatar has been in the lead, readily disgorging its gas-generated wealth in the pursuit of the downfall of the House of Assad."

"Qatar's influence over military supplies to the [Syrian] rebellion may be waning, as its role in weapons deliveries takes second place to that of Saudi Arabia. [...] Mustafa Sabbagh [...] is considered the most powerful man in the political opposition. The owner of a building material and contracting company, the 48-year-old secretary-general of the National Coalition [...] he does oversee the coalition's

budget, to which the Qataris are the biggest donors, and is responsible, as one western official says, "for writing the cheques". While seen by both friends and detractors as a shrewd man who appealed to Qatar officials' business-minded attitude, Sabbagh has come under criticism for supposedly using his position to control the opposition and further Qatari influence. [...] Claims of Qatari dominance of the opposition persisted, even after the coalition was created. True, the Muslim Brotherhood was no longer the main component, but a new bloc of more than a dozen members, brought in by Sabbagh as representatives of local communities in Syria, sparked new disagreements. It was seen as another bloc that was loyal to Qatar. Each of these members was supposed to represent a local council in Syria's different provinces, and together the councils received $8m from Qatar soon after the formation of the coalition. Qatar was also the first – and possibly the only – country to provide funding for the coalition budget, to the tune of $20m, and it delivered the first $10m out of a pledged $100m package for the organisation's new humanitarian assistance unit." [36]

---

[36] https://www.ft.com/content/f2d9bbc8-bdbc-11e2-890a-00144feab7de

In the beginning of the revolution, there were a lot of analyses by speakers and writers explaining the intervention of Qatar and its axes with stories about gas and oil pipelines. There were a lot of rumors which gave the impression that that was the story, which the Syrian rebels didn't mind. For them, they wanted to topple the Assad regime at any price. They wanted to end these long decades of dictatorship and knew that it was impossible without international help. Even if we accept such explanation, how could we explain other wars like the wars in Yemen where no gas or oil pipelines. These wars were created by same countries in the same time using the same tools and methods.

If the war was about gas or oil, Assad and Russia should and could behave in a completely different way. At least they wouldn't need to kill babies or to torture the peaceful innocents. These indications indicated that the story was somewhere else away from oil, gas or any of the similar classic goals of regular wars.

Another explanation assumes that these countries which are ruled by conservative regimes need constant "holy wars" to get rid of the extremists which might threaten their stability and legitimacy. Wars like that of Syria, Afghanistan, Iraq, Bosnia and Thailand all presented a great chance to send thousands of radical fighters to places where they would happily die.
This could also be an interesting point to western countries as well. The constant existence of holy wars contributed to the work of the western intelligence agencies in may ways, either by helping the "friend

regimes" like the Arab Gulf countries or observing the extremists and their activities. The daily scenes in the media which provoke radicals and bring them to one point, was very helpful for these services.

I will relate this point in another way so as to be clear, as it is critical in this respect. If these wars were not based on a religious or sectarian basis, they wouldn't acknowledge or attract these radical elements. If these wars were just classic wars for oil, gas or economic reasons, without daily news and scenes of rape and killing children, and without news amplified systematically, they would not attract billions of dollars in donations from all around the world. This money, which will be donated from individuals, governments and organizations, will not end up in the the Syrians' pockets or mouths. It will end up in bank accounts in Turkey or will disappear somewhere along the way.

If we go further in believing some conspiracy theories, these wars could be motivated and pushed by some complexes and cartels which profit directly from them. The bills of such wars are paid for by the tax payers of some countries, while the money ends up in the bank account of some narrow circle of weapons manufacturers and security companies.

Countries like Qatar and the United Arab Emirates are small countries with short-term experience in intelligence work. Furthermore, they have enough money and don't need to invest in such industries, i.e. the wars industry. Was their role just spontaneous reactions motivated by an adventurous attitude that developed reactively? Were they proxies to some other powers hidden behind them and instructing them?

> *"Qatar's ruling family, the al-Thanis, have no ideological or religious affinity with the Islamists – they are simply not choosy about the beliefs held by useful friends. Qatar has supported the Muslim Brotherhood in Egypt and Tunisia's Islamist al-Nahda party, which won the first elections after the popular revolts." "It is this kind of dynamism and risk-taking at an executive level that has enabled Doha to act as a regional power only a few years after being a diplomatic nobody."*
>
> *"[Qatar] hosted the US's biggest military air base in the region, while maintaining cordial relations with Iran; it held contacts with Israel while simultaneously backing the Palestinian group Hamas and Lebanon's Hizbollah."*
>
> *"One person who influenced the emir's thinking at the time is Azmi Bishara, a prominent former Arab Israeli MP, exiled in Qatar [...] An adviser to the emir and the crown prince, Bishara has become something of a court intellectual in Doha. He is said to have been involved in the formation of the Syrian National Coalition, now the main opposition umbrella group, and to have been used to "test" opposition figures. [...](Bishara was not available for comment.)"[37]*

---

[37] Ibid

The Financial Times magazine published a very interesting report about the Qatari role in Syria beginning a few years before the revolution up until the most recent events.

I will quote from this report the main milestones of this role, but I wish to draw the attention of the reader to an important issue.

What the report describes is not restricted to the Qatari behavior in Syria. When we move to study the roles of Saudi Arabia and the United Arab Emirates in countries like Egypt, Turkey, Balkan States, Yemen, etc… we see an exact similar scenario…

With some adaptation to the conditions of each country, the practices and tools are the same. These tools are mainly based on invading the targeted country with investment in media, the finance sector, espionage agents under titles like charity organizations, businessmen, and a huge tourism movement…

> ➤ *"It wasn't long ago that Bashar al-Assad and his wife Asma were regular visitors to Doha, as guests of the emir and his second wife, Sheikha Moza. Qatari institutions were big investors in Syria, with a $5bn joint holding company set up in 2008 to develop everything from power stations to hotels.*
> ➤ *The emir also championed the international rehabilitation of Assad during his gradual ostracisation by the US, Europe and his Arab peers; Sheikh Hamad was instrumental in*

restoring Syrian relations with France in the years before the uprising, when he counted the former president Nicolas Sarkozy as a friend. Back then Syria was part of an alliance – with Iran and Lebanon's Hizbollah".

➢ *"As the Arab world's bloodiest conflict grinds on, Qatar has emerged as a driving force: pouring in tens of millions of dollars to arm the rebels. Yet it also stands accused of dividing them [...] Qatar has contributed – estimated by rebel and diplomatic sources to be about $1bn, but put by people close to the Qatar government at as much as $3bn."[38]*

➢ *"But the military stalemate of the Syrian uprising [...] has also revealed the recklessness and political impotence that ultimately undermine Qatar's objectives.*
'The Qataris are overextended [...]" comments another diplomat'.

➢ *"As the Qataris have attempted to unite the political opposition by championing the formation of the Syrian National Coalition (the main front) they have been accused of dividing it – just as their efforts to shape a fragmented rebel army into a more coherent form by helping to unify the brigades under one command have contributed to its incoherence."*

➢ *"By early 2012, as peaceful protests gave way to an armed opposition, Qatar was scouring*

---

[38] Ibid

around for light weaponry, buying arms in Libya and in eastern European states, and flying them to Turkey, where intelligence services helped deliver them across the border. At first, say people with direct knowledge of the arms shipments, Qatar worked through Turkish intelligence to identify recipients, and then, as Saudi Arabia joined the covert military effort, through Lebanese mediators. The Stockholm International Peace Research Institute, which tracks arms transfers, says that between April 2012 and March this year, more than 70 military cargo flights from Qatar landed in Turkey."

➤ *"As the conflict progressed, the Qataris worked through members of the exiled Muslim Brotherhood to identify rebel factions that should be supported. For example, she says, that is how they linked up with the Farouq brigades, one of the largest and more mainstream factions. Meanwhile, opposition sources say the Qataris have also sent their own special forces to find insurgent groups, and people involved in the weapons business say a Qatari general has been the point man on arms deliveries, travelling to the "operations" room that was set up first in Istanbul and then in Ankara."[39]*

---

39 Ibid

Homicidal Frankensteins

The Role of the Media and Intelligence Agencies in the Syrian Crisis

Introduction

The telling of the story of Syria remains incomplete without going through the role of the media and international organizations. This means primarily the intelligence agencies, the military complexes, and some NGOs which are influenced and directed by the latter.

In this chapter I will describe some behaviors of these entities.

The role that these organizations played in the Syrian tragedy is not small. In one way or another, the behavior of these organizations is responsible for the massacre. It is the deadly part of the story. All other things which the media focused on were either distraction or the result of the behavior of these bodies. Without these organizations, the amount of Syrian bloodshed would not have reached such a horrible level.

But do I believe in the conspiracy or not?[40]

---

[40] In this section I will try to get free of the fear of being accused of being a conspiracy theorist or a fan of some conspiracy theory. I will tell my interpretation freely. For the readers who suffer a severe allergy in regard to any conspiratorial thinking: You have got a full explanation and facts in the first half of the book. This part I will devote for my own interpretations of these facts.

Well, here is how I see it: It is not most important to decide whether there is a conspiracy or not. No matter if events are part of a conspiracy or not, humanity urgently needs to be aware of the behavior of these organizations.

During my journey of writing this book, some friends criticized me because I skipped mentioning the "family who controls the world." Others doubted the credibility of the book because I deliberately avoided mentioning the "one organization that controls the whole world" or the role of the "small religious country which controls the world." Other critics were on the opposite side. They criticized that I write in such a way that gives the impression that I am a conspiracy theorist and advised me to change my style.

Throughout many discussions about the Syrian issue I kept coming to the same conclusion. A "conspiracy theory" is an issue which can neither be proved nor denied. It is like the question: "Does God exist or not?" I will not overload my small book going into such a question and I will leave to the reader read to interpret my observations in the way that fits their "beliefs."

The reader can explain these observations as "accidental" or that "events happened according to the nature of things." I would also never mind if any conspiracy theorist took my observations to prove their theories and complete the missing part of the story (according to them), telling the readers about the one family/organization/country who rules the world. All I want to say is that this book is devoted to the events that I experienced and were in my research area. I mentioned to the reader in the beginning of the book that the book wouldn't tell the Syrian story from A-Z. I don't think that any one book can do that. Let's say that this book only tells the story from O to P. Any work that tells the story before O or after P would be great.

Most important, the Syrian tragedy is not the last episode of this bloody series. It was not the first one either. The behavior of these organizations keeps multiplying the tragedy into unlimited copies. It is like a complicated product which needs a long time to be designed and manufactured. However once it starts to function, it quickly produces thousands of similar pieces in rapid succession. This is how it appears to me when I watch these organizations multiply what happened in Syria. It spreads to other countries like Yemen, Venezuela, Jordan, etc. The Syrian tragedy itself was an updated version of the Iraq war and before that the Afghan war.

The Behaviour of Syrian and Arabic Speaking Media

The Arabic speaking media polarized the Syrian nation telling completely different stories about the nature of the conflict. The opposition media talked about freedom, revolution, democracy, or the right of the Sunni majority to govern Syria. Meanwhile the media of Assad's regime was talking about the global conspiracy against the regime. Each party got tremendous support from its allies. The regime's media was backed by the media sources of Russia, Iran and Hezbollah. There were unlimited mercenary writers. These journalists were reporting to the Arabic speaking and international media. The landscape on the other side was not different. Media channels like Al Jazeera, Al Arabiya, and others played a big role in preparing the Syrian crowds for the revolution. This role continued throughout the years of the revolution. These media channels chose the representatives of the Syrian opposition and their speakers.

Again, I am not going to go through the question as to whether these channels acted as a part of a previous plan or if their acts were just a normal response to the events and circumstances. However, I might mention that the story of a polarizing media didn't start in 2011, but instead many years before that.

The British Broadcasting Corporation BBC[41] produced a documentary covering the phenomena of the spread

---

[41] https://www.youtube.com/watch?v=n_NKgXGcxX8

---

of sectarian TV channels. The documentary concluded that most of these TV channels were supported and financed by unknown or ambiguous founders and contributors. These TV channels are responsible for the bloodshed in Syria and many other Muslim countries.

The report stated that: "The most provoking channels produce not only from Arabic countries, rather from Great Britain […]. We observed the existence of tens of Islamic TV Channels […] Their content can't be broadcasted, it is provoking […]

The BBC team could find 120 religious TV Channels, 20 of them which broadcast provoking content. The report investigated a couple of them which are:

-   Alanwar 2 TV channel, a Shiite TV Channel. It invites the Shiite to fight in Syria against the Sunnis. The offices of this channel exist somewhere in an unknown location in Baghdad. An Alanwar executive refused to name the contributors or the financier. [Al Anwar TV is a Shiite TV Channel which was founded 2004 and broadcast from London, its headquarters is in Kuwait and has offices in Syria, the United States, Lebanon and Iran).

-   Ahl Al Bait TV Channel. This also is a Shiite TV Channel which collects money from Iraq and broadcasts from United States. Its founder is Hasan Allah Yari, an Afghani Shiite cleric who resides in San Diego, California. He is accused of having connections with the C.I.A[42].

- Safa TV. A Sunni TV Channel that broadcasts from Egypt. The BBC journalist met one of Safa's moderators and accompanied him in his "Jeep Cherokee" car to the Channel headquarters. Safa is considered one of the best equipped channels. The Safa moderator considers the Shiite doctrine a fake ideology created and financed throughout the history by Jews. The finance of Safa TV –according to the BBC journalist- is covered with the utmost secrecy. However, the BBC's investigations led to that the director and financier of the channel is actually a Kuwaiti businessman called Khaled Al Osaimi. He refused to meet the BBC team.

- Fadak TV Channel is located in very a luxurious neighborhood in the UK. The director of the Channel, the Shiite cleric Yasser Al Habib, bought an ex-church building for one million English pounds. He changed it into a mosque/TV channel studio which broadcasts 24 hours.

- Wesal is a Saudi TV Channel founded in 2009. It also has a branch in the UK. However, it broadcasts in the Persian language, targeting the Iranian masses. It is financed by Saudi and

---

[42] http://www.alkawthartv.com/news/110080

Kuwaiti money. It encourages the Iranians to revolt against their regime and topple it.

The documentary skipped reporting about one of the most influential preachers in the Syrian playground, Adnan al-Arour:
"whose fiery blasts beam across two Saudi-owned Salafist satellite channels, as a bigoted ghoul. Especially damning was footage in which the sheikh rose, shook a warning finger at the camera and vowed to "grind the flesh" of pro-regime Alawites and 'feed it to the dogs' [...]
The channels where Mr Arour has appeared devote most of their airtime to attacking Shia Islam. His dismissal of Kurdish claims for greater autonomy risked alienating a valuable component of the anti-regime front." [43].

Al-Arour didn't stop at preaching and splitting the Syrian community. His role went even further. He supervised the military operations and the financing of the opposition extremist factions.
"he starred at a rare gathering of commanders from rebel military councils, showed how popular he is among the fighters. Yet it is not just the surge in religiosity among Syrian Sunnis that gives him his cachet. Mr Arour has been a vociferous and effective fund-raiser in the Gulf."[44]

---

[43] https://www.economist.com/middle-east-and-africa/2012/10/20/the-charm-of-telesalafism
[44] ibid

The phenomena of the religious TV channels was not unique in the Syrian and Arabic landscape. There was huge investment in the media market - either in TVs, writers, or an internet platform. There was a lot of suspicion surrounding the source of financial sources of this flourishing market and if it was just natural movement responding to the market demand or it was systematic work targeting each category of the Syrian and Arabic crowds. Unlimited Media channels appeared in very short time targeting the various categories of the Syrian nation: The conservative Islamists and radicals, the Kurds, the intellectuals, the communists etc.

The work seemed professionally organized. The representatives, writers, or public speakers of each group received professional training and extra generous payments from ambiguous sources and unclear reasoning. Before 2011, no country, leading channel or newspaper wanted to host or welcome any speaker, although the crimes of the Assad regime had been ongoing since 1970. The speakers who became daily guests to the international media channels even before the revolution started were not welcome and barely appeared on the media pulpits. Suddenly they were given international screens to talk 24/7 without restriction.

In 2007, a private channel called Addounia TV was established in Syria by Rami Makhlouf, the most famous cousin of Bashar Al Assad, who got his reputation as an icon of corruption. In the same year, another private TV Channel was planned by a Sunni businessman based in Dubai. Ghassan Abboud " left Syria for the United Arab Emirates at the beginning of the 1990s, and worked in public relations in the Abu Dhabi Engineers Association Branch, and was then Media Officer in the Emirates Equestrian Federation and Race."

In 2011, Abboud was one of the first business and media men who declared their opposition publicly through a public announcement on the TV channel, the Orient News. Since then, the channel adopted the Syrian revolution as a single topic. It became the other polar on the other side of the Addounia TV Channel.

Al Jazeera, the most influencial Arabic-speaking news channel, used to praise Assad's resistance against Israel . Its moderators like Faisal Al Kassem contributed to enlightening Assad's image as a hero who helped the Palestinians in their war against the Israeli. Faisal Al Kasem used various techniques to terrorize anyone who might try to criticize the Assad regime.

Reports about the Assad regime's crime against freedom of speech or against the political activists could barely be heard on Al Jazeera before 2011. Suddenly, the tone was shifted. Who was yesterday the faithful hero of the Arabic world became the betrayer and the most dangerous war criminal. Bashar Al Assad's crimes became the central topic of the Channel, although these crimes didn't start in 2011. The dictatorial and criminal behaviour of the Assad family had not stopped since they came to the power 1970.

This applies to many other media channels. After 2011 the Arabic media shifted to promote and enlighten Erdogan and Turkey. Erdogan was introduced as an inspired Muslim leader who would restore power to the Muslims and their international position they enjoyed in the past. Praising Turkey and polishing Erdogan's image became an "essential daily meal". The exact moderators who enlightened Assad and demonized him were later those who worked on enlightening Erdogan's image and demonizing his enemies!

In 2000, the Saudi TV Channel MBC produced a TV Show based on an old Arabic story. The main concluding quote of the "Al-Zeer Salem"[45] story says: "don't make peace". Bab El Hara[46], is another Syrian TV Show and one of the most popular Arabic ones. The first season was produced in 2006. The TV shows gained exceptional popularity. Al Jazeera TV Channel reported a "curfew"[47] in some Arabic countries during its episodes because the people stayed at home to watch it. However, the TV show was criticized by the intellectuals for imposing an historical fake image of the Syrian community. The TV Show gave the Syrians some values, mainly emphasizing the necessity of a stubborn attitude while fighting against the enemy. It also discouraged any rational thinking about the wars or revolutions, no matter how great the loss.

---

[45] http://www.imdb.com/title/tt3109706/
[46] http://www.imdb.com/title/tt1999065/
[47] http://www.aljazeera.net/news/cultureandart/2007/10/10/باب-الحارة-يفرض-حظر-تجول-على-الفلسطينيين

I observed the techniques that the media used to manipulate the Syrians during and before their crisis. I later observed the European and western media and concluded that the manipulation techniques used by these media are not different.

Thanks to the role of these media channels, Syrians who lived together for decades ended up as complete strangers. In a few months the anti and pro-Assad Syrians became enemies and couldn't trust or believe each another anymore. This plan was applied again in the opposition areas based on ethnic, ideological or sectarian factors. This was how the extremist areas were made to be so different from the moderate ones. The ultra-extremists started to defect from the less extremist ones and attack them. The Kurdish opposition didn't want to stay in sync with the Arab Opposition. The media worked on splitting these groups into smaller ones based on tribal, regional and other bases.

The Behaviour of the Western Media

Throughout the years of the Syrian crisis, the mainstream media explained the western failure as just a series of accidental mistakes, mere confusion and a lack of experience. This sounds to me simply not convincing. The western intelligence agencies have demonstrated a high performance level in many other events. It reached a very sophisticated level of organization and knowledge decades ago. Further, unintentional confusion can't continue for many years like it did in the Syrian case and other similar cases like in Iraq, Yemen, Afghanistan and others. The bill of each of these failures is estimated to be millions of victims. It is mysterious when these intelligence agencies become suddenly helpless and amateur.

Sibel Edmonds, the Ex-FBI agent illustrated this phenomenon when she described a similar case while she was employed by the FBI:

> *"Yassin Al Kadi was one of our guys, CIA guys, with the Turkish Network together, having these terrorist related operations going on. But every time FBI wanted to go and snatch the guy, the State Department and the CIA would step in and they wouldn't let it happen. Then we had 9/11 taking place, and this was when we had Robert Wright coming out talking about it*

and saying: "they stopped the investigation", the United States government. We had one of the financers. Okay? And they didn't let us pursue him. They didn't let us capture him. So, by this time Al Kadi was actually declared, even by the United States, that yes, he was in fact the financier. But, even after he was declared they gave him, the United States government, enough time to pack his stuff and go to Albania. It was like "oops" too late we can't catch Al- Kadi he's gone. So he continued his operation. Again, This is the operation Gladio B, with the Turkish operatives in Central Asia, in Caucasus out of Albania. Then, of course they dragged their foot. This is the United States State Department worldwide declared him as the financier of 9/11 and a wanted man. And they said oh he's in Albania and we are going to request Albanians to turn him over. We have his address everything right? Well they made sure it took about two weeks between the time they asked requested Albania until he actually went to Turkey. And again in Albania he had Albanian passport. In Turkey he was already a Turkish, resident there. So he left Albania and U.S. said "oops" we couldn't catch him in Albania. He is not there any longer. He is in Turkey. So the United States told Turkey, they said (you know, knock knock, wink wink): "we want you to give this guy's back. We want him here. He is one of the top financers of 9/11. And we know that the in Turkey you don't even take a piss without the green light and permission from the United States. Turkey, for the first time ever, told the United States: "we don't have extradition treaty with you, and he hasn't violated any Turkish laws. We are tough. We are a very tough nation and we're not gonna hand him over to you." and the United States said: "oh okay" and the case ended. Now Al Kadi, actually he has ownership in several banks in Turkey including in Cyprus. And meanwhile he's going to Azerbaijan and again we covered the stuff at Zawahiri. You're looking at the same operation team, you're looking at. And he stayed there for years okay? and meanwhile he's also travelling globally not only to Azerbaijan. He's going to London for his business matters.

And he got some top attorneys and basically told the United Nation: "you need to undeclared me as a terrorist". So the United Nations took him off the list and U.S. basically covered up this whole thing. How could this guy in Turkey running this operation which is for United States for the CIA operations in Central Asia and Caucasus and the issue was completely covered up? As you know, the media here in U.S. never really covered Al Kadi. You won't find more than handful of articles. And suddenly, lo' and behold with Erdogan they leaked the fact that, here are the pictures of Erdogan's sons getting into this ten or 20 million dollar deal with Al Kadi, the al Qaeda top financier. Here is the partnership between this member of our own family and Al Kadi who is Al Qadea's top financier. And that's exactly what we are seeing."[48]

During the Syrian crisis years, the mainstream media overwhelmed their followers with daily reports and explanations similar to the above story narrated by Sibel Edmond. I would call this kind of narrative the "oops" effect. It is a modern generation of manipulation and one of the most dangerous tools used by the media to distract the crowds from what is really going on.

Doubting such a narrative might lead to thinking in a "conspiracy theory" way. However, in my opinion, the insistence to believe all these "oops" and the abstinence from posing any question about them is even more stupid than thinking about a conspiracy.

Here are some samples: "The United States committed to arm the Syrian opposition to topple Assad, but

---

[48] https://youtu.be/q32-2sMzrWw

"oops", it turned out that there are extremists out there. This surprised the American officers. It was not known to them before." "The western countries sent billions of financial aid to the Syrian opposition, but "oops" it turned out that the Syrian opposition members were corrupted." "The western countries wanted really to topple Assad's Regimes, but "oops" it turned out that the opposition was divided and the leaders didn't want to unify."

Here I will quote again what Dr. Nikolaos Van Dam noted:

> *"Donor countries (like United States and Turkey) sometimes simultaneously gave contradictory instructions to Syrian military commanders in battles with the Islamic State, threatening to stop their military aid if their instructions were not followed up. Syrian commanders also complained about the lack of relevant military intelligence, which could have been provided in time by their foreign supporters, and about lack of sufficient ammunition (which they occasionally described as a kind of "drip-feeding"). Opposition commanders sometimes felt betrayed."*

> *"Western criticism of the military opposition, concerning a lack of coordination, was*

*therefore unjustified insofar as this was a result
of a lack of Western military coordination"[49].*

*"The Qataris and Saudis were creating
separate military alliances and structures.
[...] Commanders who work with Idriss say
that neither country is following through with
its promise to bolster the supreme military
command, instead continuing to work
independently. [...] "Qatar and Saudi Arabia
... are playing out their rivalries here, they are
dividing people," says Abdul Jabbar Akaidi,
the head of the Aleppo revolutionary military
council." [50]*

The opposition members that the western entities
blamed for the failure are the ones that these entities
chose. Nobody chose these members of the opposition
but the western intelligence services themselves. The
Syrians didn't choose them. No election or even
referendum was held to choose them. No single Syrian
was consulted about choosing them. There were plenty
of other choices, but the western intelligence agencies
assigned these exact figures out of thousands other
choices. For choosing these figures, the western
entities adopted the exact standards which were
applied by Assad's regime and Al Baath Party for
decades when it comes to choosing the officers and

---

[49] Destroying a Nation: The Civil War in Syria, by Nikolaos Van
Dam, pp 2018.
[50] https://www.ft.com/content/f2d9bbc8-bdbc-11e2-890a-
00144feab7de

agents. These standards simply are: The absolute loyalty and Obedience, the readiness to report and do espionage work for the sponsors, and most importantly, to be corrupt-able. Honest elements are not appreciated here. Throughout the crisis years, these members continued their corruption in public, without any inspection by the donor countries. These are the same countries which monitor their citizens so closely that they know when they commit a tax fraud of ten bucks. This behavior of the western intelligence agencies was not a fad in the Syrian case. The exact same scene was witnessed during the Iraq war51.

The above described "oops" way of manipulation is the exact inversion of "Aha effect". Only when we reject believing these frequent "oops", we might get to the "Aha" effect and start to understand what is going on.

---

[51] Read the Guardian article "How the US sent $12bn in cash to Iraq. And watched it vanish:
The US flew nearly $12bn in shrink-wrapped $100 bills into Iraq, then distributed the cash with no proper control over who was receiving it and how it was being spent."
Refer also to the book: "Pay Any Price: Greed, Power, and Endless War" by James Risen, pp 2015 ISBN: 978-0544570351

The media traps:

The "Oops" way of manipulating is not the only manipulation technique used in our time.

I consider manipulation as the most homicidal weapon in our time. The reason why I think so is: There are few people in the world that are in favor of the continuance of wars. How could the warlords still start these wars against the will of the majority? The answer is simple: With manipulation they can!

During the Syrian crisis years, I could observe and define many suspicious media behaviors and tactics which were used to distract the crowds from what was really going on or what should have been done.

Telling the crowds what they want to hear, not what is really going on

This sort of manipulation could be inherent to the media. The media does not necessarily practice such manipulation deliberately or consciously. It just responds to how people interact and react and what they would like to hear. The crowds are interested in listening to facts which back their view or their ideas about life and the world.
The western audience, for instance, would like to believe that Middle Eastern nations are, finally,

rebelling for their freedom. This came from their paradigms surrounding a historical development and their own view of life. They project their own history on current events and recall events like the French Revolution and the World War harbingers. The intellectual Syrians wanted to hear only this exact story. They ignored any other facts. The Salafists in Syria and in the Arab Gulf countries would like to hear a completely different story. They preferred to see the revolution as a rise of Sunni Islam against the Alawite or secularity. Each party found a media which responded to their wish and repeated the story that fitted their liking. The truth of what was going on was not important for any party.

But how much does it really matter to know the real reason and trigger of wars?

The importance of knowing "why the war starts" lies in the fact of "unless we knew the reason for the war, we wouldn't be able to finish it."
All mankind has tried to stop wars but it has resulted to be useless...
War-lords can let the media explain the reasons for wars by telling unlimited stories about the Sunni-Shia conflict, Dictatorship-Freedom conflict, Kurdish-Arabic conflict, and Turkish- Russian conflict. They also could talk about conflict over gas and oil, profit conflict between the Russian axis and NATO, competition between Saudi Arabia and Iran, between Capitalism and Socialism, or drought and desertification, Star Wars, Harry Potter, whatever...

These reasons have existed for ages. I don't deny here the fact that they are there. I just claim that they didn't cause a war until "war-lords" used them to launch wars all over the world according to their own demand and profits. The media entertains its audience with what they would like to hear, while the war-lords complete the process by profiting from these wars and adding fuel to the fire. The point is: none of these reasons CREATED the war, the real creators and their motives hide somewhere out of this landscape and are rarely mentioned.

The media tends to talk about persons or events: Saddam Hussein, Bin Laden, 9/11, Deraa's children, Tunisian policewoman, etc. while the real reason(s) for the war are somewhere else... The wars in our age represent the ultimate edition of organized crime, and it is not about men or events. Even if Assad dies the next morning (or his whole family, Putin or Erdogan), the war or crisis won't end because it is not about them...

But even this illusion and misunderstanding doesn't come spontaneously... In the Syrian war (for instance), thousands of sponsored social media groups and accounts, video channels, news agencies, and figures were devoted to keeping eyes on "persons" or events... focusing their eyes on some clan, sect, or party, while spreading news implying that these symbols were in their last days... By using this technique (among others), the Syrians (all fighting parties) have lived 8 years (so far) expecting that the end of the war will happen soon, while the country has been destroyed and gradually disappears!

'WE CAN'T SOLVE PROBLEMS BY USING THE SAME KIND OF THINKING WE USED WHEN WE CREATED THEM'

ALBERT EINSTEIN

Overwhelming the crowds with irrelevant details and narrative

This kind of manipulation is used almost all the time in our media, in the tabloids as well as more reputable sources. It distracts its audience with names, personal behaviors and minor details.

We have to realize that we live in the age of international poles and axes. History can't be decided solely focusing on the views of individual people or groups of people. Countries are now connected to each other and the superpowers won't allow personal behaviors and views to threaten their interests or to risk the world order on which they worked. Some media tries to convince us otherwise by telling us unlimited irrelevant stories.

Some media tends to explain international events based on people such as Donald Trump, Kim Jong-un and so on. Other media explain huge events based on single events, while the real triggers of the events on the international stage lie somewhere else. Noam Chomsky explained this idea by saying once:

"Trump's role is to ensure that the media and public attention are always concentrated on him. So every time you turn on a television set: Trump, open the front page of the newspaper : Trump, you open the front page of the newspaper: Trump. He's a conman, basically a showman and in order to maintain public attention you have to do something crazy, otherwise nobody's going to pay attention to you. If you do

normal things you'll be way back somewhere. So every day there's one insane thing after another and then you know the media, he makes a crazy lie, you know, he had the biggest crowd in history or something, then the media looks at it and says 'No, that isn't the biggest crowed', but meanwhile he's on to something else and then you go to that one and while this show is going on in public, in the background the wrecking crew is working. Paul Ryan, Mitch McConnel; the guys in the cabinet who write his executive orders, what they are doing is systematically dismantling every aspect of government that works for the benefit of the population, this goes from workers' rights, to pollution of the environment, rules for protecting consumers, I mean anything you can think of is being dismantled and all efforts are being devoted, almost with fanaticism, to enrich and empower their actual constituency, which is super wealth and corporate power. "[ii]

The Pepsi VS Coca-Cola trap

In this trap the media serve their audience two options as if there is no third one. It raises endless disputes in which people try day and night to prove which choice is better. "Who is the liar, the Western or Russian media?" "Is NATO good or the Putin-Assad-Iran axes"? "Should we destroy Iraq, or close our eyes and turn our back leaving the Iraqi tyranny to kill whoever he wants?"

As if the rejection of one option necessarily implies acceptance of the other.

However, but we need in each incident sort of answer, correct?

Correct!

There are always unlimited possibilities and answers. Nevertheless the media distracts the crowds from seeing any third answer or even posing a third question.

In a world that we would hope for, it is not acceptable to leave a tyranny to slave or kill its nation. I have a complete disregard towards what "legal experts" wrote in the constitution of the UN Security Council.

The alternative option is not necessarily delegating to one or two entities like the CIA or the British military complex to destroy a nation without any responsibility. The presidents and directors who dictated the invasion of Iraq or the operations in Syria were not investigated. The victims of this behavior in each case are in the millions.

This trap played a homicidal role in the Syrian crisis. Many intellectuals, thinkers and even academic scientists fell in this trap. A wide range of the western audience found themselves in a pre-taken attitude and biased to Assad's side. They refused to believe any reports about the Assad regime's crimes against millions of civilians. Assad's media and its allies, mainly the Russian, Iranian and their public relations arms made great use of this trap and profited from it until its last edge. After the Iraq war, the global mood was against any similar war. The media uncovered a lot of manipulation used by the western media to justify the war against Iraq and the Saddam Hussein regime. In the Syrian crisis this meant that the crowds automatically adopted the attitude of defending Assad and tending to hear only good things about him. This enabled Assad's regime to go in brutality to the most severe edge. The crimes which were committed by Assad's regime could exceed what the Nazi regime did in World War II.

The role of Social Media:

The entities which sponsored TV channels, newspapers and other propaganda tools were of course aware of the modern tools like social media.

The social media platforms were used heavily during the Syrian crisis. The Arab spring might not arise without these platforms, mainly Facebook, Twitter and YouTube.

The role that the social media platforms played was not completely or necessarily part of a "conspiracy".

Here is an example that illustrates why it is difficult to decide if the events happen naturally or as a part of a conspiracy, and what we should do towards that.

Platforms like Facebook or even the online stores are responsive. This means that they observe the behavior of the consumer and respond in the future accordingly.

When a customer buys a political book from Amazon, it is expected that Amazon would suggest them other political books in future.

The same can be said for Facebook, Twitter, Youtube and so on...

It is understood that the platforms adopt such quality. The commercial logic implies that.

However, this responsive quality is responsible for polarizing the communities and nations in a very dangerous way.

Imagine that 2 neighbors use social media for couple of hours every day or buy their stuff online. One of them might like, perhaps accidentally, a few funny images of cats or they might have bought a few books about gardening. The other meanwhile "liked" or "shared" a few posts about dogs or might have bought some science fiction books. Here is what will happen afterwards. The book stores and social media will show each of them thousands of similar material according to each one's behavior. It will not take more than a few months until these two neighbors become strangers. Each one wouldn't be aware of what the other is talking about or in which planet they live.

It is difficult to claim here that it is a "conspiracy". However, mankind should be aware of this danger and deal with it as if it were a homicidal conspiracy.

This can split nations, create wars, and isolate families and inhabitants.

Some organizations could make out of this point unlimited wars and conflicts. All they need is a budget and to be free from values or ethics.

Besides the normal accounts which belong to individuals there were the sponsored ones. These accounts played a big role in shaping the collective minds and leading them in specific directions.

Some of these accounts behave in suspicious way. It is clear and easy to recognize that they were created systematically and used all the platforms' possibilities as if their creators were trained to do that in a professional way. Part of this job was discovered later[52]. Others declared their activity as a part of solidarity[53].

It is completely understood that the security services wouldn't spare using artificial intelligence and social media to observe the crowds and spread targeted ideas. Before the social media revolution, these services used other techniques like Radio, word of mouth propaganda and rumors to achieve the same goals.

---

[52] Like Cambridge Analytica https://www.theguardian.com/us-news/2018/mar/23/john-bolton-cambridge-analytica-videos-donald-trump
[53] Like the Syrian Electronic Army https://www.politico.com/blogs/media/2013/08/what-is-the-syrian-electronic-army-171438

The Role of the Intelligence, Security, and Military Complexes

Introduction

In the Iran-Contra Affair "the National Security Council (NSC) became involved in secret weapons transactions and other activities that either were prohibited by the U.S. Congress or violated the stated public policy of the government." [54]

"It was planned that **Israel** would ship weapons to Iran, and then the United States would resupply Israel and receive the Israeli payment." [55]

The president at the time, Ronald Reagan, "gave the impression of knowing little of what was going on." Several investigations were conducted. Neither found any evidence that President Reagan himself was aware of the multiple programs' details.

"The funds were first sent to Saudi Arabia"[56]. The Saudi businessman "Khashoggi was an important middleman in the arms deals behind the Iran-contra scandal" [57].

---

[54] https://www.britannica.com/event/Iran-Contra-Affair

[55] "EXCERPTS FROM THE TOWER COMMISSION'S REPORT
"http://www.presidency.ucsb.edu/PS157/assignment%20files%20public/TOWER%20EXCERPTS.htm

[56]
http://content.time.com/time/magazine/article/0,9171,157496,00.html

[57]
https://www.nytimes.com/2017/06/06/world/middleeast/adnan-khashoggi-dead-saudi-arms-trader.html

When we reflect upon this issue[58], we come to notice a few interesting details:

The relations between the main players of this scandal were severely complicated. Iranian officials and citizens called the United States at the time "The Great Satan" and Israel "the Small Satan". It was not unusual to hear declarations like "Israel should be annihilated". The percentage of Iranian citizens who shared this view with Iranian officials was not small. The feelings that the Israelis and Americans harboured against the Iranians were not much different.

When we talk about Saudi-Israeli or Saudi-Iranian relations, the landscape looks similarly messy.

How can these countries meet and sign sensitive agreements when they are sunk in such grudge oceans? When we try to describe the relations between countries, we have to differentiate four different levels of power:

1. The ordinary citizens who are not directly involved in political decision-making.
2. The officials, i.e. the technocrats, ministers, government officers and so on. This level is supposed to care about the interests of the whole nation. However, the views and values of this level are not necessarily the same as that of most citizens.

---

[58] This is not a unique case in the modern history. The modern history is full of discovered cases. The undiscovered are even more. However, I will use this case to illustrate differentiation we need to understand the international events of modern history.

3. The military complexes and intelligence service agencies[59].
4. A small circle of leaders and key persons who direct the military complexes and intelligence service agencies.

Of course, the four levels described above are not completely disconnected from each other. Important to remember here is: **the relations between the countries at each level don't necessarily reflect the relations at other levels.**
Just because the individuals of two countries have peaceful feelings towards each other, that doesn't necessarily hold true for other levels. Vice versa, when war is declared between some countries, that doesn't mean that the relationship between these countries' top level power centers are in the same state of conflict.

---

[59] Some parts of my writing might sound like a "conspiracy theory". I have to admit that this is a problematic issue. It is difficult to decide if these organizations behave as a part of a "conspiracy" or they just act and react accidentally according to the natural development of things.
 While some "conspiracy theories" sound sometimes silly to many readers, believing that all these things happen just accidently in cases sounds to me to be not that much smarter.
Here I need to make it clear. I didn't start with any theory or pre-judgement. I am not interested in proving any conspiracy theory. All what you will read came based on my observations and based on facts. I will devote this section to describe my observations that match similar cases in other wars. Some examples of these wars are Iraq, Rwanda and others. I will also mention some observations of which I am not convinced of the generally accepted story or they sounded to me illogical.

What we need to keep in mind is: the interests, values and views of each level are not the same. Thus, we shouldn't talk about them collectively. Otherwise we would end up misunderstanding a lot of political issues today. It is too easy to be manipulated and fooled.

When we say "the Americans invaded Iraq" we are committing a paradigm mistake, one which led to huge misconceptions. What happened was: the top level of decision-makers in the United States made the decision to invade Iraq. This means that the majority of Americans were not invading but were rather victims of this invasion. Furthermore, the US decision-makers responsible for this invasion conspired with figures from Iraq itself. These Iraqis were not among the invaded, but were in fact part of the invasion.

Thus, the contradiction in international politics is not always between nations, i.e. Americans against Iraqis. Rather, the contradiction in many cases lies between, on the one hand, the politicians of all nations, and on the other, the general citizenry of those nations. Correcting this misconception is the first step towards understanding modern political events, and to finding solutions for the soaring wave of wars.

How and when did these organizations get to their unique position?

The acquisition of power by these bodies was not accidental. It happened gradually throughout history. It was an evolutionary process with roots going back to the middle ages and ancient times. However, this process witnessed its most dramatic leap during the world wars of the twentieth century[60].

Until World War II, history was still based upon the sole decisions of dictators, kings and princes. World War II itself was –apparently- triggered, then driven and developed out through the unique perspectives, actions and reactions of persons like Hitler, Stalin, Churchill and others[iii].

However, these dictators and rulers invested heavily in improving security services during World War II. There was no other option at that time. They were interested in defeating the enemy at any price. They handed to these services all nations' resources and possibilities. They also assigned many tasks to these organizations. These entities became not only espionage and military organizations, rather they

---

[60] "Following the outbreak of war with Germany in 1914, the Foreign Section worked more closely with Military Intelligence. [...] This was a period of dramatic growth and change for the Service, but its work had a major influence on the eventual victory." Retrieved *on 09.06.2018* from the British Intelligence Service, MI6's official website: https://www.sis.gov.uk/our-history.html

expanded their work to include propaganda, media control, and crowd observation.

Since the World War II, these bodies have gained exceptional tools to retain their position as independent decision makers. These services gained organizational capabilities and structures that made them independent from the technocrat rulers. Their structure allowed them to maintain their power even after the wars ended.

These mechanisms are a mix of legal, political, and financial tools. There also exist loopholes along with media "tricks." Most important they have a wealth of studies, unlimited historical case studies and experience. In a phrase, there is a wealth of information.

Mechanisms which were created at that time guaranteed them these exceptional privileges to the present. They have now their own view which doesn't necessarily comply with the view of the majority of individuals or even with the technocrat politicians. Presently they are not now mere administrators for their countries' leaders. They have an organic independent life on their own apart from their creators.

Later the intelligence organizations in the superpower countries developed similar structured organizations in the third world. The superpowers' security services transmitted, conditionally and partially, part of their wealth of knowledge, experience and organizational capabilities to their counterparts in the third world. This way, the services in the developed world kept their domination over the third world. They own the knowledge which controls the crowds of these nations and they transmit it to specific groups which comply with their policies and goals.

Where do the superior capabilities of these entities come from?

Historically, the human groups who were one step further in owning specific knowledge could dominate and control those who were one step behind.
Some nations who owned the knowledge about gunpowder, though they were far fewer, controlled other continents.

What knowledge can justify the superior position of these organizations over a nation?
Perhaps the long term accumulated and intensified knowledge over the short life-long divided ones.
The power sources of these organizations come mainly from focused information and a profound experience accumulated in key fields. These fields include propaganda, control of the media and public perception.

Individuals can't build airplanes or operations systems. Only huge organizations can. These organizations use the knowledge and experience of thousands of scientists accumulated across decades or even centuries, focus them in one project, then it could be done.

However what kind of products do such organizations deal with?

Here is the first tricky part of the story. While companies like Apple or Tesla rush to tell us about their products even before they produce them, the intelligence forces invest in products that they are keen not to talk about. These products, if they would ever have names, they would be training programs called something like: "how to control minds" or a book called "how to influence nations' opinions and direct them", or software called "how to divide a nation, create a war and profit from it."

If this is true, why don't the common people of a nation gain the same knowledge?
Here is the second tricky part in the story. When the nations were controlled by people using gunpowder, the people of the controlled nations actually knew that they were controlled. They strived to learn the nature of the control in order to restore their freedom. Those who are controlled by subtle weapons like manipulation, media or mind control don't know that they are being controlled or manipulated. That is why they don't have any motivation to learn about the nature of modern control.

The Science of Creating a War

"If the newspapers begin to publish stories about wars, and the people begin to think and talk of war in their daily conversations, they soon find themselves at war. People get that which their minds dwell upon, and this applies to a group or community or a nation of people, the same as to an individual." Andrew Carnegie, circa 1908

"The Prince" was written in the early 16th century. In this book, **Niccolò Machiavelli** explained a series of "tips and tricks" to contemporary leaders in order to teach them how to control nations and dominate crowds.

The title came from the principal person that Machiavelli wrote to, hoping for some favoritism. It could also be titled, "How the prince should behave to stay prince".

However, if such book was written in our time in the United States, a completely different title would be chosen for it. It could be called something like, "How to dominate nations and control the crowds," or "Controlling nations for dummies" or something similar.

The author would become a consultant and start big consultancy firm. He would start to target the wealthy governments who are thinking day and night how to maintain their superior position. The book could be taught in training programs. If the writer lived in Silicon Valley, he might consider developing an app called "how to control crowds."

If billions of dollars were invested to develop apps like Tinder or video games, how much money would you expect to be invested in such an app?

The business related to such products is not estimated in the billions of dollars, rather in trillions of dollars[61]. But who might be the users of such an app? Who might be the students of such a program or the readers of such books?

Here is how Anthony Robbins described his experience when he worked with *the U. S. Army and the* CIA:

> *"Years ago, I had the unique opportunity of working with the U. S. Army, with whom I negotiated a contract to reduce certain training times for specialized areas. My work was so successful that I also went through top-secret clearance and had a chance to model one of the top officials in the CIA, a man who'd worked his way up from the bottom of the organization. Let me tell you that the skills that he and others like him have developed for shaking another person's convictions and changing their beliefs are absolutely*

---

[61] The Three Trillion Dollar War: The True Cost of the Iraq Conflict, by Linda J. Bilmes and Joseph E. Stiglitz. ISBN: 978-0393334173.

astounding. They create an environment that causes people to doubt what they've always believed, and then give them new ideas and experiences to support the adoption of new beliefs. Watching the speed at which they can change someone's belief is almost scary"[62]

The more artificial intelligence (AI) technology gets better, the gap between these Frankensteins and the common masses get bigger. Here is how Alon Ben David, defense reporter describes this view

"How Israel Rules The World Of Cyber Security" "We're talking about here is a total revolution of the whole concept of war it changes everything we thought about war and how it's been conducted and what are the rules and who is the enemy and can you recognize the enemy at all many countries have very dangerous cyber tools some are using it viciously like the Russians like the Chinese and are not shy of using them against other countries we all understand the vulnerabilities of critical infrastructure and we all understand the vulnerabilities of privacy but what troubles me is the ability to affect the mindset of masses the mindset of Republic the

[62] "Awaken the Giant Within" by Anthony Robbins, 2001. ISBN-13: 978-0743409384

Russians were manipulating American public mindset that's scary and that I suspect would eventually undermine most of Western democracies in the coming decade I fear that the good 70 years post World War two of prospering democracies in the Western world and prosperity economic prosperity are over!"[63]

[63] in a VICE News Report https://www.youtube.com/watch?v=ca-C3voZwpM

Conclusion

So, to sum up my claims: the Syrians who demonstrated against their corrupted regime in 2011 had the fairest reasons to do so. This situation was invested by devil powers to create and start the ugliest war in modern history.

I claim here that the war in Syria was CREATED and DIDN'T just happen. I provided many incidents and proofs which indicate clearly that it was planned and intended in coordination among the parties who pretended to be enemies on the international stage.

My claims also imply that the war's parties didn't fight to win or to acquire land or natural resources. Instead, they created this war to profit from the war itself. None of them were interested in finishing the war in its early stages, even as a winner!

The bottom line executers of this war (the fighters from both sides, pro-Assad and opposition) were not necessarily aware of the real game. They received instructions from upper levels. They didn't have a chance to disobey these instructions. The upper levels which instructed them were intelligence agencies which managed this war and profited from it in various ways which I broke down throughout the book's pages. The super powers kidnapped the rebellion by picking specific opposition figures and supporting them according to these super powers' standards and considerations while marginalizing (isolating) the rest and excluding them.

The major implementers of the war, Russia and Turkey, profited economically from the war in various ways. Other parties of the game have achieved political and Intelligence goals, mainly Arabic Gulf countries, Iran and of course, the western super power countries. The major result of this game was domesticating the Syrian nation along with many other nations.

***

At one point, the whole world seemed to be watching the poor Syrians being thrown into the holocaust. But many of them, including many Syrians, were praying that these poor could be enough oblation to achieve their ambitions and dreams. All parties seemed to rely on these poor:

The west thinks that they deserve to dominate Syria more than Russia, Iran and co. the Wahhabis Gulf States think that Syria should belong to the conservative Sunni world, not to the western or the Shiite. They hoped that the Syrian children limbs would be enough to restore Syria from Iran and Russian grip.

The Conservative Muslims in diaspora, especially in the west, continue encouraging those in the Assad region to continue this collective suicide in the hopes that this will lead to their dreams coming true: an Islamic state in Syria.

The Muslim brotherhood members who are now receiving open budget financing from the west under the title of "projects" which end nowhere but their pockets and accounts, are enjoying the good life in

Turkey, hosted in luxury residency in Istanbul and other capitals, and financed unlimitedly by declared and undeclared sources, hope that these sacrifices are enough to take their revenge from Assad's regime.

The Syrians which belong to big or rich families in diaspora are convinced that they deserve more power and wealth than the Assad family. They spend their days and nights encouraging those who are still inside to go further, shaming them for being reluctant or hesitant to jump into this Holocaust. They hope that the sacrificing of these poor Syrians is enough for them to come back one day to restore their lost glory.

Even the liberal and secular Syrians who fled Syria after 2011 always have time to chant and appreciate the death and suffering of those who are inside. Enjoying the privileges which some hosting countries provide to their "guests", this category always has time to celebrate the sacrificing of those which didn't have enough sources to flee Syria. They keep assuring them that Victory is undoubtedly coming soon.

The intelligence agencies of the western super powers didn't spare any of the above categories to imply their agendas.

The media, mainly those financed by anonymous western sources, have hypnotized the Syrians with thousands of daily broadcasts on social media and other media channels.

The doping process was systematic. Thousands of writers from all walks of life were paid and financed to keep the feeling of the approaching victory alive.

Even irrelevant events like the suing of one of Assad's officers who would not leave Syria in front of some forgotten European court, freezing Assad's money in some banks, sanctions against Iran, all these events were taken by those channels and converted to indications of the "nearing fall of the regime".

Thanks to this hypnosis work, the Syrians lost any logical thinking or efficient calculation. While losing all they owned, what they inherited from the previous generations, they never stopped believing that they were the winners.

Where this hypnosis process was successful was in distracting the Syrian crowd from the essential question, which is "HOW".

How would this regime be toppled?
Even when half of the nation left Syria and the regime restored control of 90 percent of the country; even when the only fighters who remained fighting Assad were the Islamist foreigner fighters, which most of the Syrians in diaspora consider unreliable mercenaries instructed by some foreign intelligence agencies or even by the Assad regime itself; the Syrians in diaspora continued talking daily about the victory which was no doubt coming. This seemed to be not only a case of hypnosis, but rather severe schizophrenia.

The speakers, writers and journalists who were part of this hypnosis work received huge financial support, mainly from Qatar and Saudi Arabia, and other western countries, mainly the United Kingdom and United States.

This systematic work had one goal: to distract the crowds from stopping to reflect and going on without discovering the game until it was too late. And this devil plan worked out unbelievably successfully, one must admit!

***

Syria is an open wound. It is not possible to say: "That is all about Syria, The End". Thanks to our current technology, it is possible to write a book and put it in the hands of millions, while retaining the right to always add new discoveries, views and experiences on a daily basis. Thus, I would like that the reader stay tuned to the updates of the Kindle edition of the book (which is free when buying this paperback from Amazon).

www.sytruth.com
https://www.facebook.com/truthinsy/
info@sytruth.com

SINCERELY,

WASEEM KANJO

VIENNA – 2018

TO THEM:

The victims of the war princes, who couldn't find another business except these children's blood, limbs, future, and dreams.

APPENDIX

FURTHER READING AND REFERENCES

[i] **10 June 2011** Erdogan, Speaking on Turkey's ATV channel, said: "The situation in Syria for Turkey is not like that one in Libya, Syria is almost like an internal affair (for Turkey). We have an 800- to 900-kilometer border. We have relatives there. Turkey can't accept repeating Hama massacre. http://archive.arabic.cnn.com/2011/syria.2011/6/10/turkey.syria/

Two years later, Erdogan would appear again repeating the same monologue. At that time, the Syrian victims of this "play" exceeded triple the number of Hama massacre. Though, Erdogan didn't seem to be regretful or excusing. He rather looked like an actor who played his role perfectly.

This play has continued with the same momentum till the moment of writing these lines. The propaganda channels, which are financed mainly by Qatar, didn't stop praising him as "the leader who didn't let the Syrians down". This continued non-stop during the 8 years of the Syrian tragedy, even after 600,000 were killed, 10 million were displaced and unknown amounts of damage and loss.

19 Aug 2011, Obama said "Assad must resign"
"U.S., Europe call for Syrian leader al-Assad to step down"
"Secretary Clinton Says Syrian President Assad 'Must Go'"
http://edition.cnn.com/2011/POLITICS/08/18/us.syria/index.html
https://www.theguardian.com/world/2011/aug/18/syria-assad-must-resign-obama
https://abcnews.go.com/Politics/secretary-hillary-clinton-syrian-president-assad/story?id=16049737

May 16, 2013, "Obama and Erdogan: Syria's Assad Must Go"
Wall Street Journal,
https://www.youtube.com/watch?v=rvvqrwwkSlM

The speech was just after Obama's so called "red line" was crossed, in which Assad reportedly used the chemical weapons as the American investigations have proved.

"I have, at this point, not ordered military engagement in the situation. But the point that you made about chemical and biological weapons is critical. That's an issue that doesn't just concern Syria; it concerns our close allies in the region, including Israel. It concerns us. We cannot have a situation where chemical or biological weapons are falling into the hands of the wrong people.
"We have been very clear to the Assad regime, but also to other players on the ground, that a red line for us is we start seeing a whole bunch of chemical weapons moving around or being utilized. That would change my calculus. That would change my equation."

"In April, in a letter sent to lawmakers saying there was evidence that chemical weapons had been used in Syria, White House legislative affairs director Miguel E. Rodriguez asserted"
https://www.washingtonpost.com/news/fact-checker/wp/2013/09/06/president-obama-and-the-red-line-on-syrias-chemical-weapons/?utm_term=.9b44b8dda9ac

[ii] Prescribed from Noam Chomsky interview, https://www.youtube.com/watch?v=uQvig0KvUaE

[iii] Dictators improved the work of the intelligence organizations to meet the complicated challenges of modern international political realities. However, many facts played a role in helping these organizations reach this ultra-unique position:
-   The democratic changes in almost the entire world, which reduced the powers of presidents and kingsiiiiii.
-   The complicated work of decision making on an international scale. Modern technology made it necessary that decisions are be made based on long-term studies and experience, rather than the view of dictators.

- This profits achieved because of this business proved to be the most important work, which achieved more than any other sector.
- The huge and dramatic leap in the business size and concept. This leap was parallel to revolutionizing changes in science capabilities and scale.